ARIA

KOZUE AMANO PRESENTS.

VOYAGE 1

Welcome to
Neo-VENEZIA

CONTENTS

ARIA VOYAGE.1

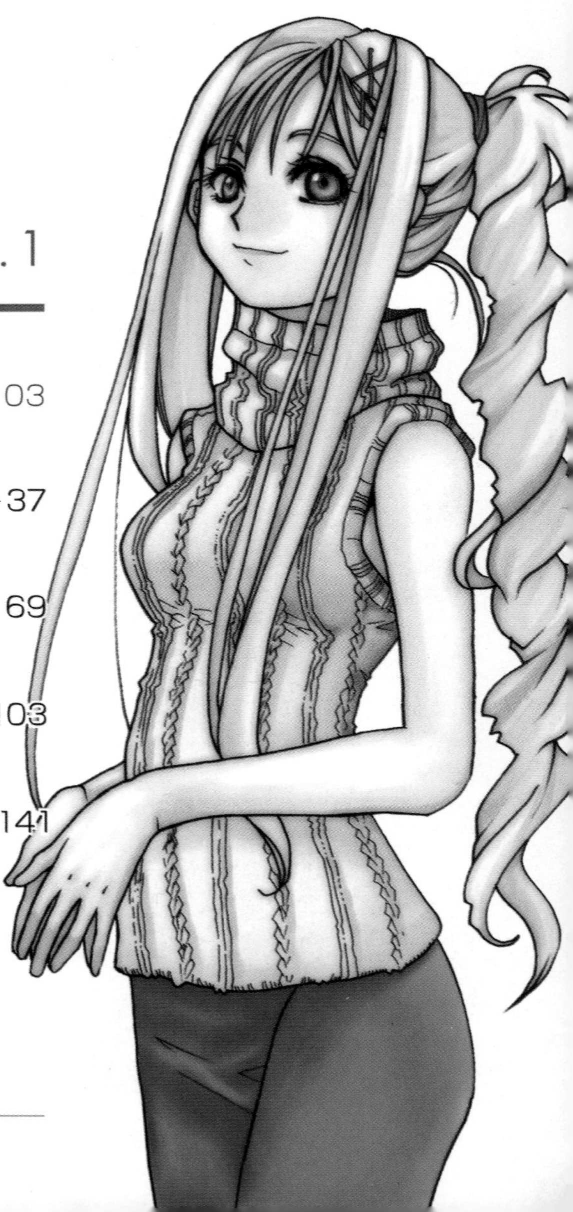

LIVE
EARTH - MARS

TODAY, WE'RE BROADCASTING LIVE FROM THE WATER PLANET, AQUA.

GOOD MORNING, PEOPLE OF EARTH!

GAM 07:36

THE PROCESS MELTED THE POLAR ICE CAPS MORE THAN EXPECTED, COVERING 90% OF THE PLANET'S SURFACE WITH WATER —— WHICH IS WHY IT'S NOW KNOWN AS "THE WATER PLANET."

IT'S ALREADY BEEN 150 YEARS SINCE THIS WORLD, WHICH WAS ONCE CALLED MARS, WAS TERRA-FORMED.

ONE WITH A UNIQUE **PROFESSION** THAT ENCAPSULATES THE VERY **ESSENCE** OF THE CITY...

NEO-VENEZIA IS A YEAR-ROUND TOURIST ATTRACTION,

WE'RE HERE TODAY TO INTRODUCE YOU TO THE PORT TOWN OF **NEO-VENEZIA**.

THE CITY'S ARCHITECTURE IS BASED ON AN ACTUAL TOWN IN ITALY, ONE WHICH EXISTED UNTIL THE MID-21ST CENTURY.

THESE PEOPLE ROW ACROSS THE WATER, GUIDING PASSENGERS THROUGH THE AQUATIC CITY THAT IS NEO-VENEZIA.

THEY ARE CALLED: **UNDINES.**

BEEP

THERE'S ONE NOW. LET'S GO AND HAVE A TALK WITH HER.

4

Navigation01
NEO-VENEZIA

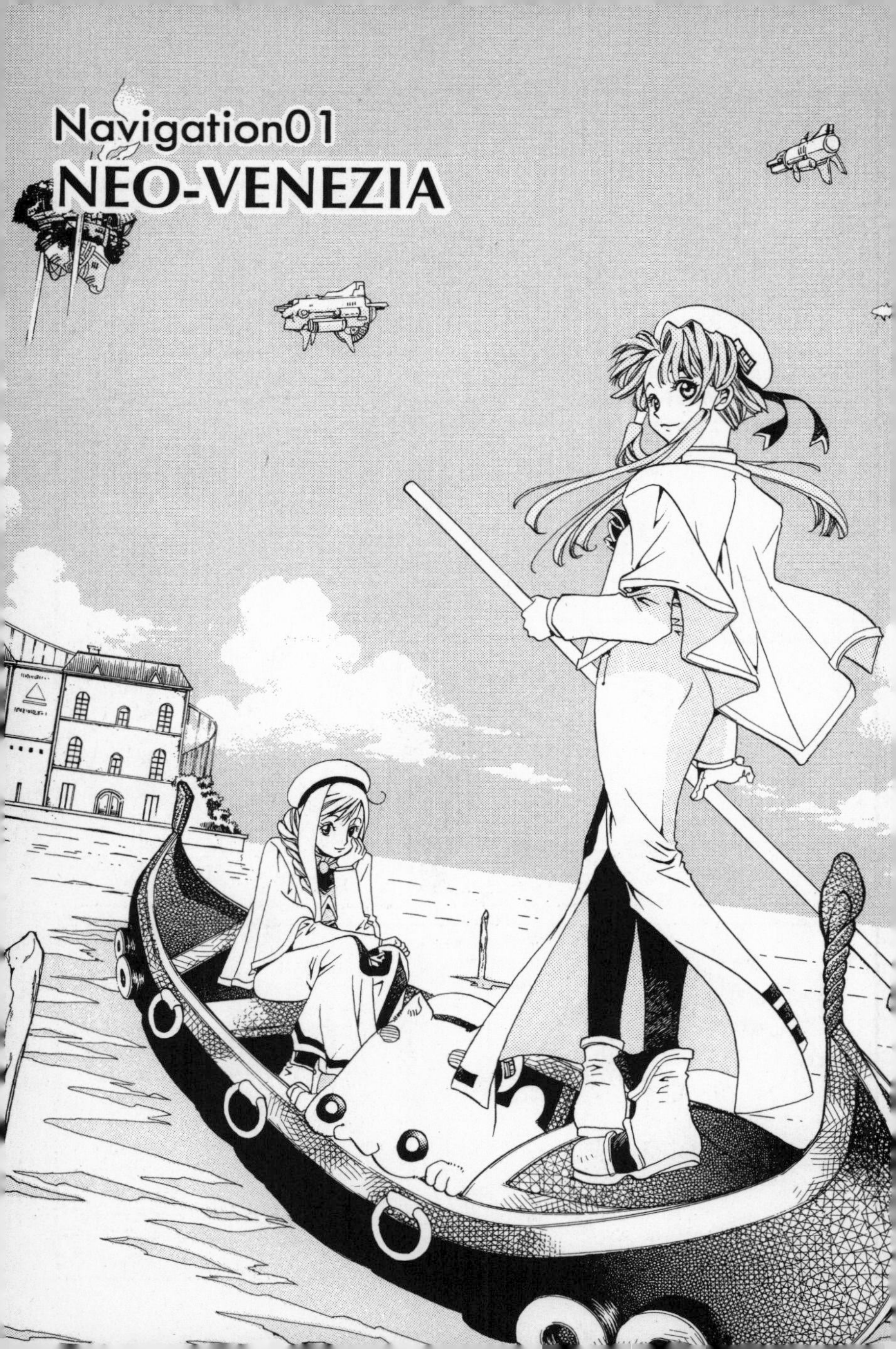

HELLO. HOW ARE YOU?

ALL THE UNDINES HERE ARE SO...

CLICK CLICK

ANYWAY. THIS IS MY FIRST AUTUMN...

ON AQUA.

IT'S HARD TO BELIEVE IT'S ALREADY BEEN

ELEVEN MONTHS SINCE I CAME TO AQUA TO BECOME AN UNDINE.

THE COMPANY I WORK FOR, ARIA COMPANY, SWITCHED TO WINTER UNIFORMS TODAY.

SPEAKING OF AUTUMN, PEOPLE START CHANGING TO WARMER CLOTHES THIS TIME OF YEAR.

Chuckle Chuckle Chuckle Chuckle

BUT I THINK I'VE GOTTEN TO LIKE THE WINTER UNIFORM, TOO.

I REALLY LIKED THE SUMMER UNIFORM,

AKARI!

HAVE YOU CHANGED YET?

FLINCH

WOW, LOOK AT YOU!

ALICIA...

OH, MY!

YOU'RE SO CUTE!

ka-chk

ONE OF THE PEOPLE I WORK WITH IS NAMED ALICIA. SHE'S ALWAYS NICE TO ME.

I'M STILL NOT VERY GOOD.

WHEN SHE HAS THE TIME, SHE HELPS ME WITH MY ROWING.

BYE FOR NOW. I'LL WRITE AGAIN SOON.

AKARI MIZUNASHI. OCTOBER 1, 2301.

RUSTLE

ALICIA, I HAVE TO GO MAIL SOMETHING.

NYU!

YOU WANNA COME TOO, PRESIDENT ARIA?

SHP ストン

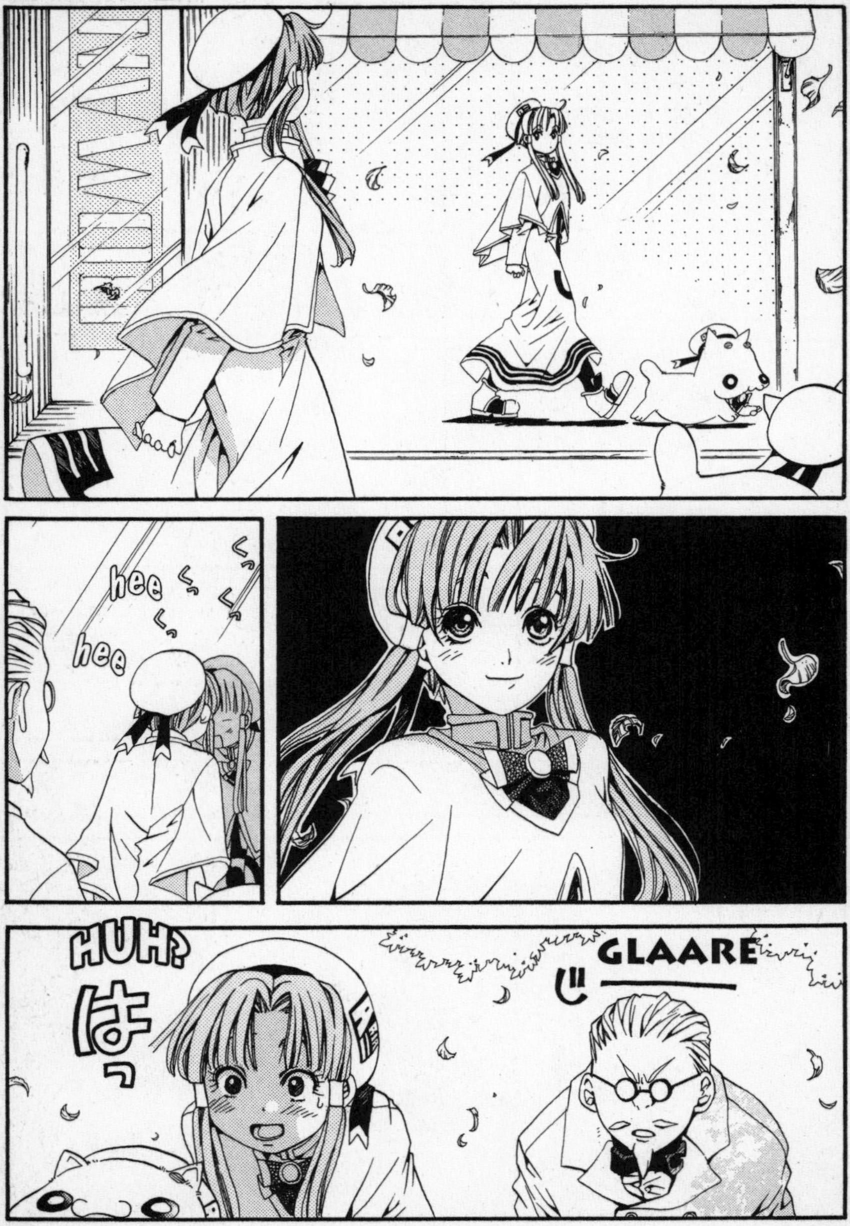
hee
くっ
くっ
くっ
くっ
hee
GLAARE
じー
HUH?
はっ

I SEE...
NONE AROUND
HERE, EH?

IS THERE
A POLICE
STATION
NEARBY?

CAN I
HELP
YOU?

SIGH...
はー

I KNOW
WHERE ONE
IS, BUT IT'S
PRETTY
FAR.

I SEEM TO
HAVE LOST MY
DAUGHTER
AND HER
HUSBAND.

IF YOU GET SEPARATED,
YOU SHOULD JUST STAY PUT, BUT...

UM, SIR?
WHAT'S THE
MATTER?

. . . .

I CAN'T BELIEVE THIS.
HOW MANY TIMES DID I TELL THEM TO STAY WITH ME?!

ずん

ずん

THUP

THUP

I COULD HELP YOU FIND THEM, IF YOU WANT!

UH, ARE YOU HERE SIGHTSEEING?

NO, THANK YOU. I'M IN A HURRY.

I MEAN, YOUR **DAUGHTER** COULD GET LOST.

IF YOU KEEP WALKING, YOU COULD GET EVEN **MORE** LOST.

THE STREETS HERE CAN BE A LITTLE CONFUSING.

WELCOME TO NEO-VENEZIA, THE CITY OF WATER!

I'M PRETTY FAMILIAR WITH THIS TOWN.

I'M AN UNDINE.

I'M GONNA CHEW THEIR EARS OFF!

WELL, THEN. I'LL TAKE YOU UP ON YOUR OFFER.

BUT AQUA'S ORBITAL PERIOD IS **TWICE** THAT OF EARTH, SO THERE ARE 24 MONTHS IN A YEAR.

HEY!

WHICH MEANS IT'S THE 19TH MONTH OF THE YEAR RIGHT NOW.

LOOK, I...

AQUA'S ROTATIONAL PERIOD IS 24 HOURS, THE SAME AS **MAN HOME'S** – I MEAN, **EARTH'S.**

I DIDN'T ASK YOU TO GIVE ME A TOUR!

FWIP!

BUT, SIR...

CAN YOU JUST CONCENTRATE ON FINDING MY FAMILY?

CONFOUND THESE LEAVES!

FLUTTER

FLUTTER

15

FORGET IT. MY TIME IS **FAR** TOO VALUABLE.

ENJOY THE AUTUMN COLOR OF THE LEAVES.

YOU'RE HERE FOR SIGHTSEEING ANYWAY, SO YOU MIGHT AS WELL MAKE THE MOST OF IT.

GRUMBLE GRUMBLE

YEAH! EVERY UNDINE COMPANY IN THIS TOWN HAS A BLUE-EYED **CAT** AS ITS BUSINESS SYMBOL.

IT'S A GOOD LUCK CHARM FOR SAFE BUSINESS OPERATIONS.

NYU

IT'S BEEN RUBBING UP ON ME...

WHAT **IS** THIS THING?

PRESIDENT?

OH, THAT'S PRESIDENT ARIA, FROM THE COMPANY THAT I WORK FOR.

NO, NOT AT ALL!

OF ALL THE RIDICULOUS...

ARE YOU KIDDING ME?

A TRAINEE, HUH?

GRUMBLE イライラ GRUMBLE

HMPH むんっ

I MIGHT STILL BE A TRAINEE, BUT I'D NEVER MAKE UP A STORY LIKE THAT!

I'M ALLOWED TO CARRY PASSENGERS

AS LONG AS I'M ACCOMPANIED BY AN INSTRUCTOR.

NYU

WAIT, A TRAINEE ?!

OH, YES !!

DO YOU KNOW WHAT YOU'RE DOING?!

SIGH はぁ―

OF ALL THE IRRESPONSIBLE ...

I **REALLY** DON'T THINK I COULD LIKE IT HERE.

THE WHOLE THING'S JUST A WASTE OF MY TIME...

GRUMBLE GRUMBLE

EARTH, OF COURSE.

MUMBLE

SO, WHERE ARE YOU FROM?

OH, REALLY?

I KNEW IT! I'M FROM EARTH, TOO!

WAY INCONVENIENT!

IT SURE IS!

I SEE.

CLEANING, LAUNDRY, COOKING...

EVERYTHING HAS TO BE DONE MANUALLY.

YES, SIR!

WHAT A BOTHER.

ISN'T IT **INCONVENIENT** LIVING IN A PLACE WHERE EVERYTHING IS A CENTURY BEHIND EARTH?

WHAT WERE MY DAUGHTER AND HER HUSBAND THINKING?

WHY WOULD SOMEONE SPEND ALL THAT MONEY ON AN INTERSTELLAR VACATION...

JUST TO COME TO SOMEPLACE SO **BACKWARDS**?

WHY DON'T THEY BUILD A MORE SENSIBLE SYSTEM LIKE THE ONE ON EARTH?

AND WHAT **IS** WITH THIS TOWN'S WATER CHANNELS?

YEAH. YOU COULD NEVER GET LOST IN AN EARTH CITY, COULD YOU?

THIS IS ABSOLUTELY RIDICULOUS!

INDEED! I HAVE **NEVER** WASTED SUCH TIME WANDERING AROUND LOST ON **EARTH.**

BELIEVE IT OR NOT, I STILL GET LOST IN THIS TOWN SOMETIMES.

HEY, HEY!

UH-OH

OOPS

I MEAN, MY DAUGHTER. GOT LOST.

?

HERE IN NEO-VENEZIA!

THINGS LIKE THAT HAPPEN ...

PRESIDENT ARIA?

SHAKE SHAKE

BE QUIET.

UM, SIR?

SHAKE SHAKE

GRRRR

EHEHE... UM, HOW ABOUT A SIDE TRIP?

WHAT ?!

BAKED POTATOES

!

LOOK, WHAT THE-?!

GRUMBLE!

I'M BACK!

WHAT **IS** THIS PRIMITIVE-LOOKING STUFF?

IT'S A BAKED POTATO.

IT'S SOOOOO GOOD!

IT'S OUR TREAT

....

AND HERE'S SOME FOR YOU!

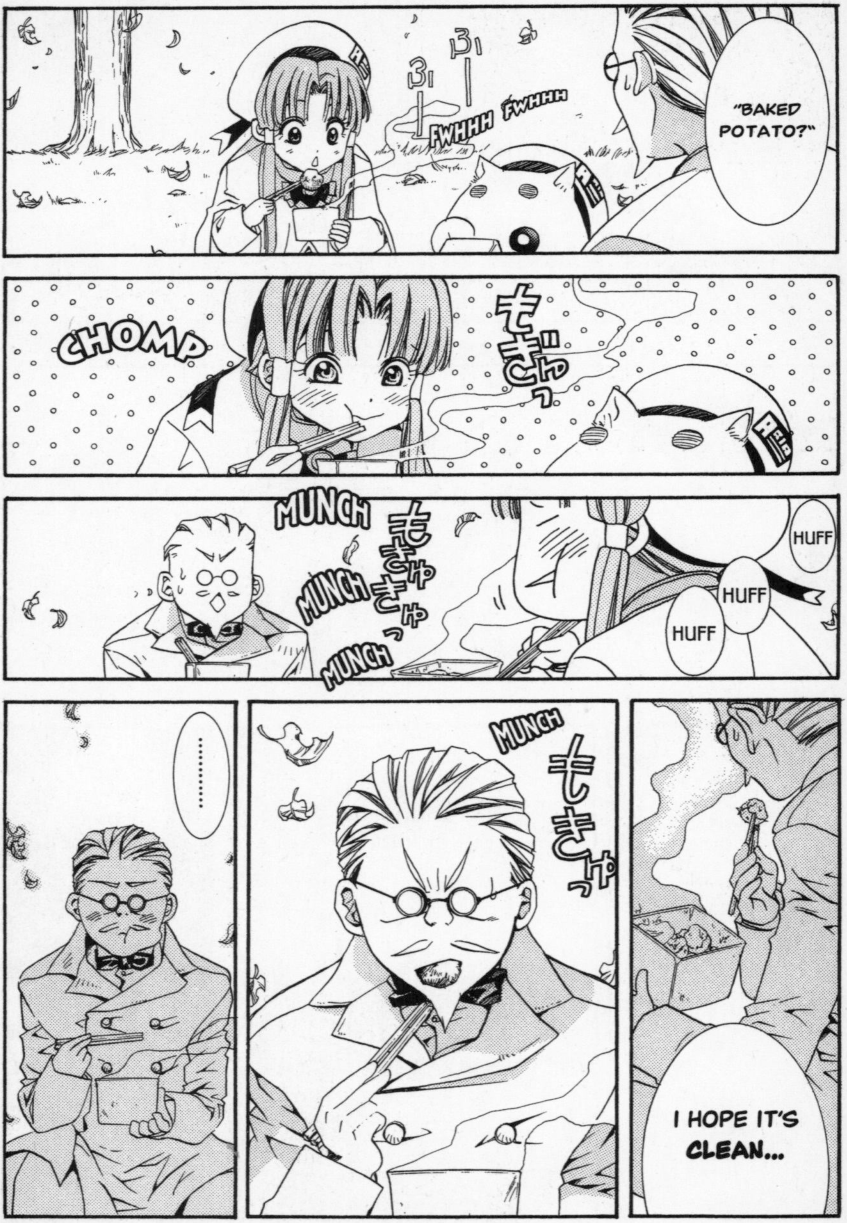
"BAKED POTATO?"
FWHHH FWHHH
CHOMP
MUNCH
MUNCH
MUNCH
HUFF
HUFF
HUFF
I HOPE IT'S CLEAN...
MUNCH
......

POP!

MUNCH

MUNCH

MUNCH

IT'S HOT GREEN TEA

HERE YOU ARE!

HUFF

HUFF

・・・・・・

SLRRP

WHY **DO**
YOU LIVE IN SUCH
A BACKWARD
PLACE AS AQUA?

HUFF

LIKE THIS ON
MAN HOME.

BECAUSE
NOWADAYS,
YOU COULDN'T
FIND A GREAT
BAKED
POTATO...

BECAUSE IT'S SO "BACKWARD" HERE THAT YOU HAVE TO DO PRETTY MUCH EVERYTHING BY HAND.

HMM... WHAT ELSE?

AND FOR SOME REASON, I KIND OF LIKE IT THAT WAY.

RUSTLE

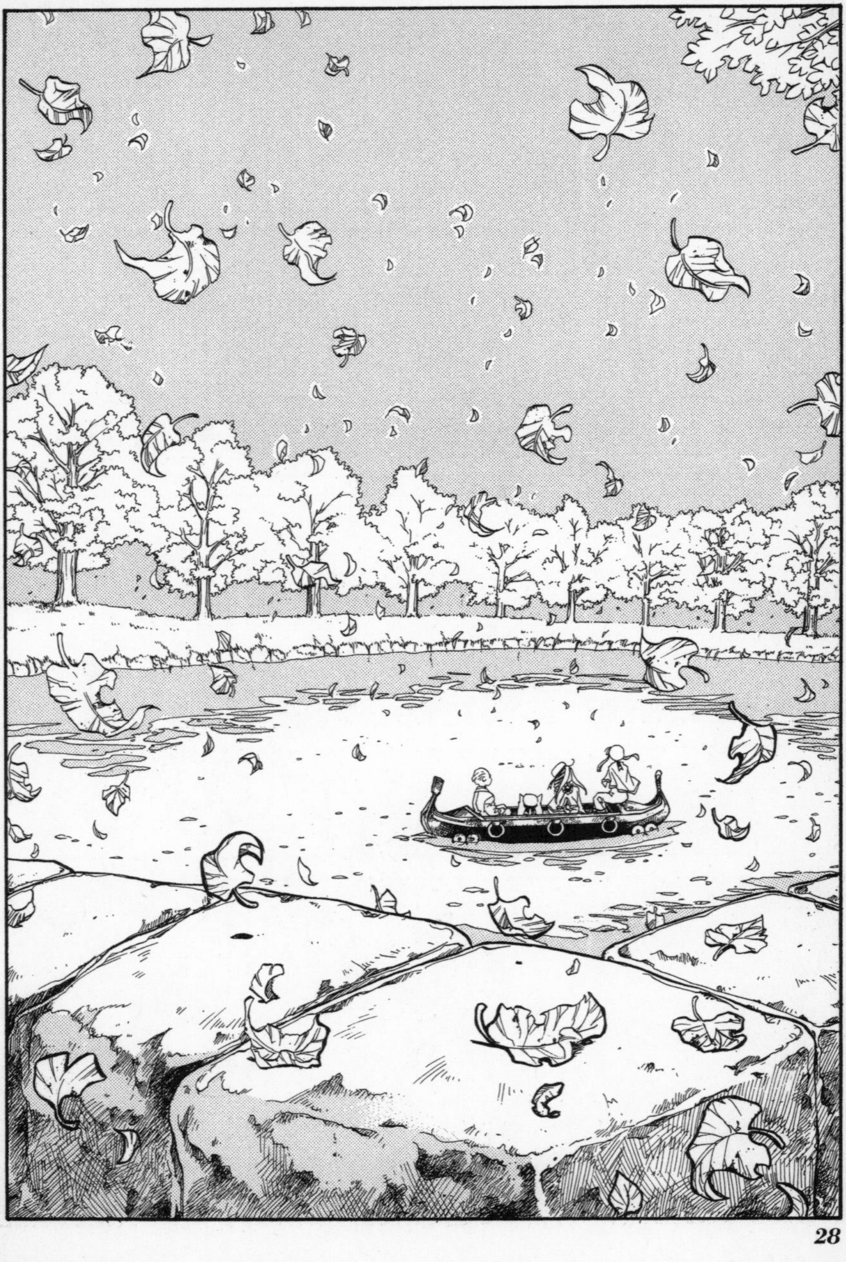

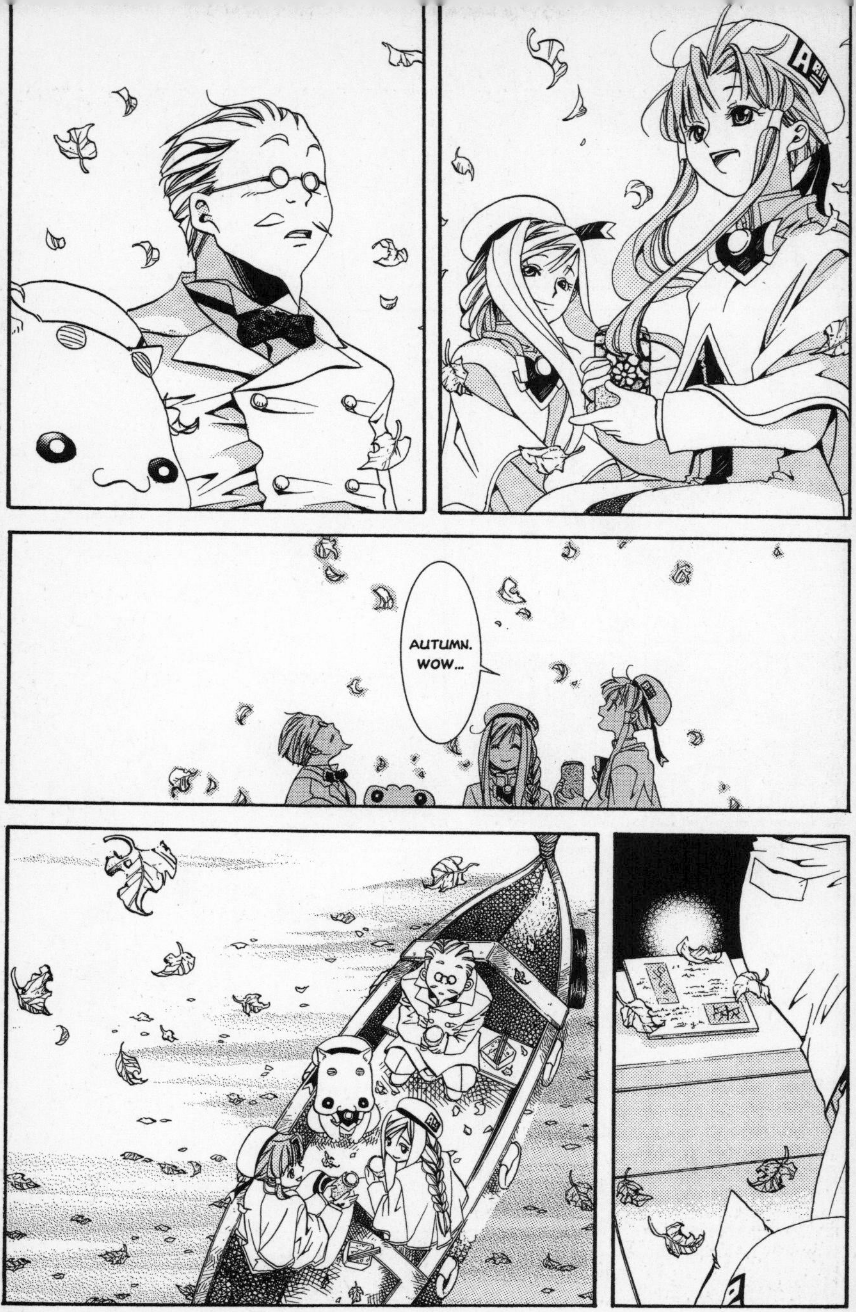
AUTUMN.
WOW...

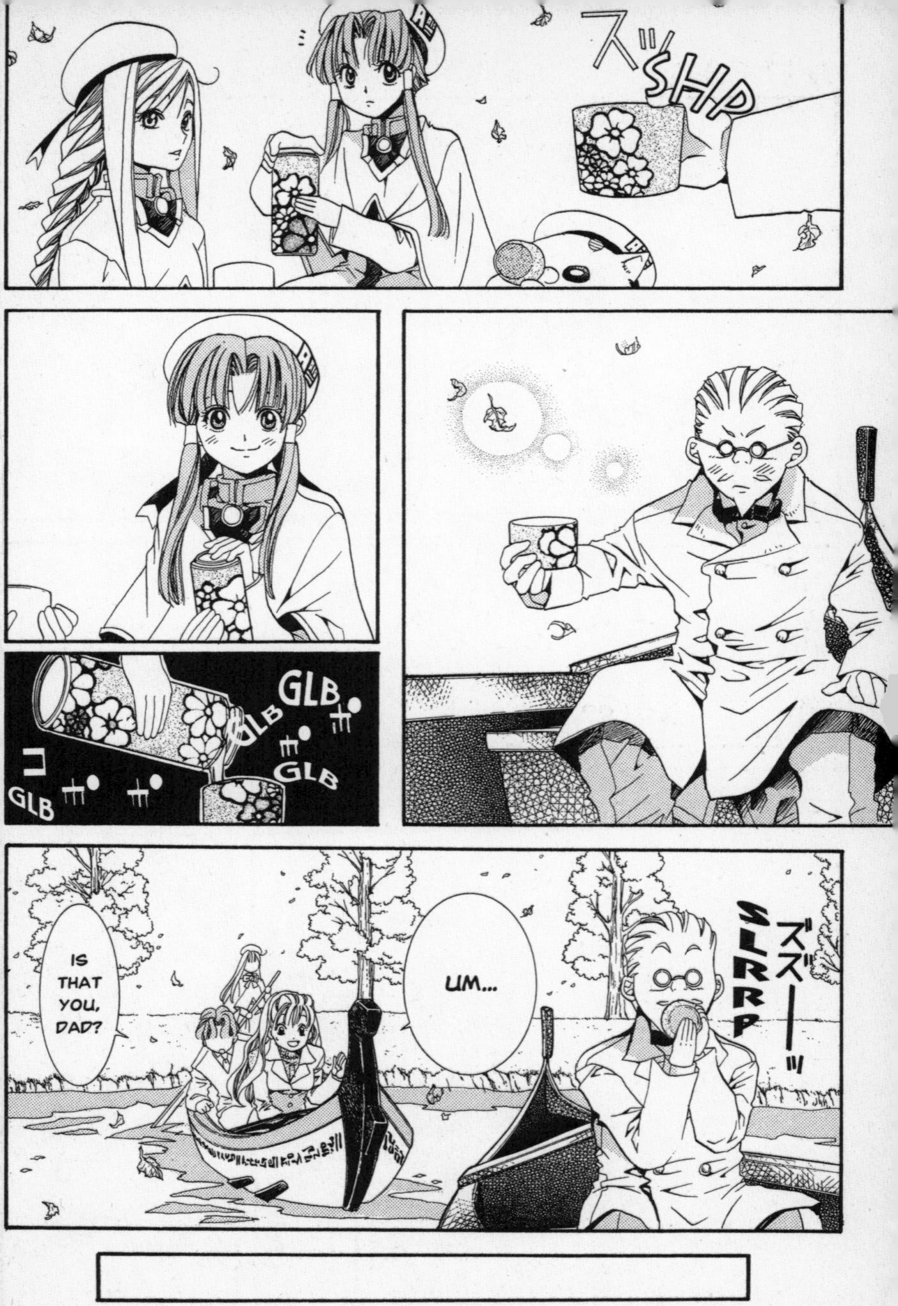

ズッ
SHP
GLB
GLB
GLB
GLB
ズズーッ
SLRRP
UM...
IS THAT YOU, DAD?

HE'S SO HARDHEADED.

I WASN'T LOST!

SO SHUT UP.

I KNOW IT WASN'T EASY FOR YOU, DEALING WITH MY **LOST** FATHER.

REALLY, THANK YOU SO MUCH.

NO PROBLEM!

HAVE A NICE TRIP.

WELL, WE'LL BE LEAVING NOW.

I DIDN'T GET YOUR NAME.

WHAT IS IT? IF YOU DON'T MIND ME ASKING...

CREAK

HEY, YOU.

WELL...

IT'S AKARI MIZUNASHI.

MISS AKARI MIZUNASHI. YOU WIN.

I THINK I'LL BE BACK SOMETIME... FOR SOME MORE BAKED POTATOES.

I'M SORRY?

YOU'RE A WONDERFUL UNDINE, YOU KNOW.

AND I'LL ASK YOU TO GIVE ME ANOTHER TOUR.

WE UNDINES MEET ALL KINDS OF PEOPLE.

ARIA COMPANY

FWSSHHH.

I'M HAPPY TO JUST HAVE THE CHANCE TO **MEET** THEM.

OF COURSE, WE DON'T GET TO SPEND MUCH TIME WITH THEM, BUT...

34

I'M REALLY GLAD I CAME TO AQUA TO BECOME AN UNDINE.

AND...

CLICK

ARIA COMPANY

THINGS ARE PRETTY GREAT FOR ME RIGHT NOW.

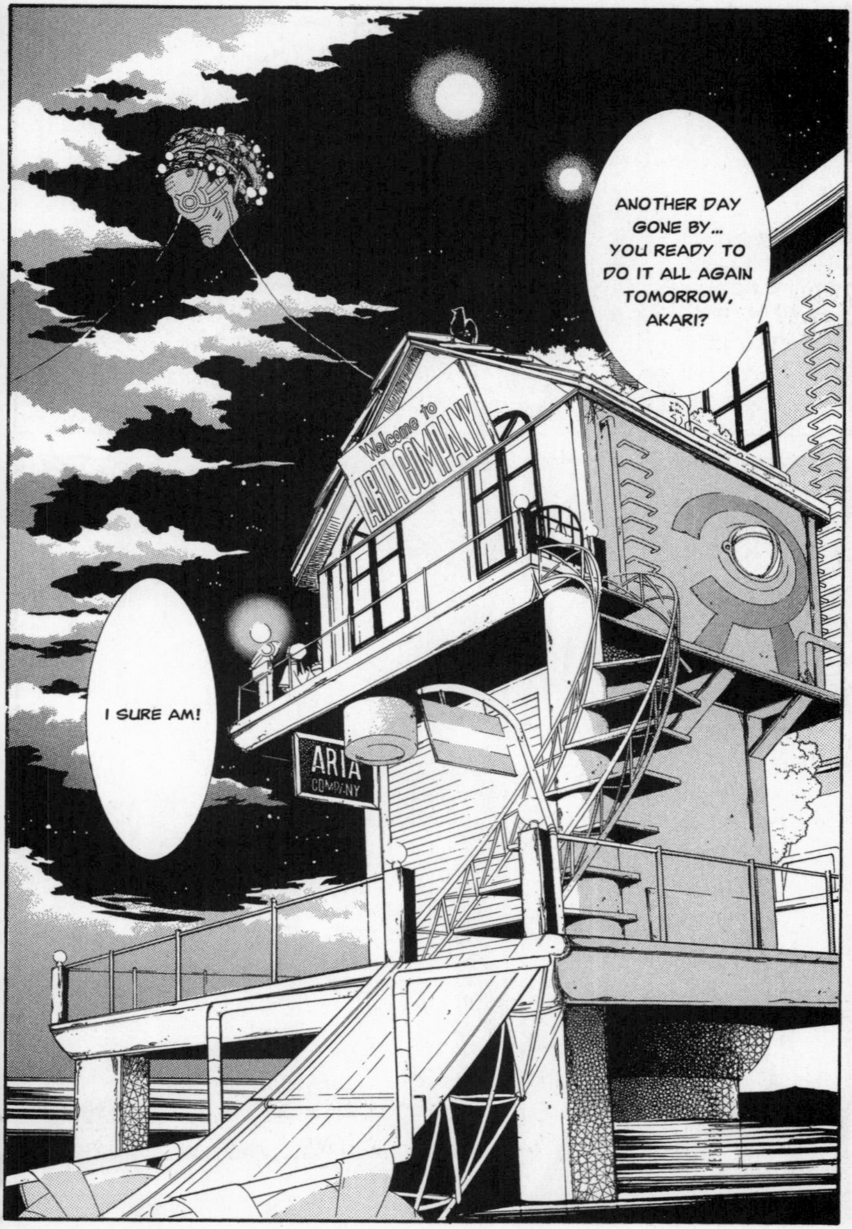
ANOTHER DAY GONE BY... YOU READY TO DO IT ALL AGAIN TOMORROW, AKARI?
I SURE AM!
Welcome to ARIA COMPANY
ARIA COMPANY

Navigation02 DRYDOCKING

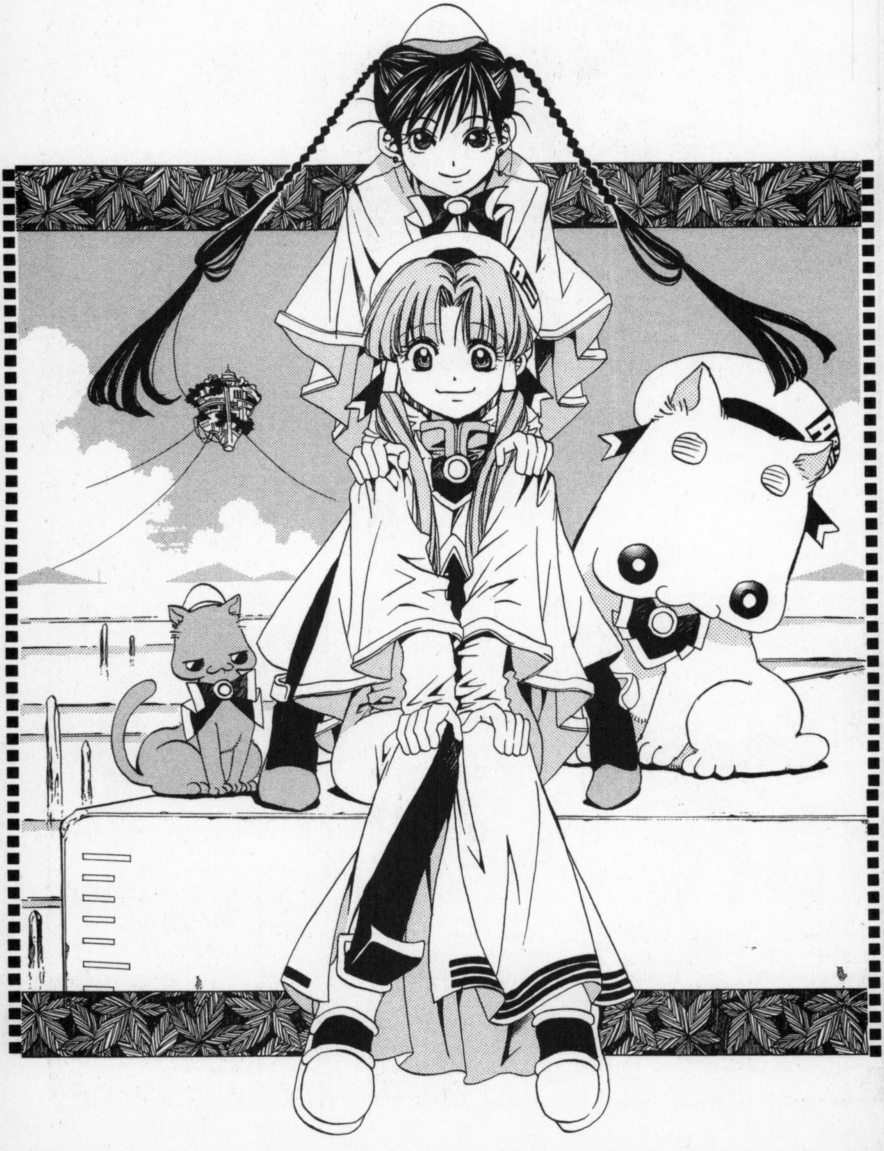

HNGRR
むー？

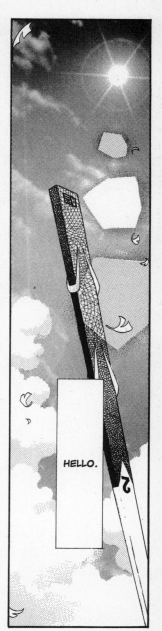

HELLO.

HM. GOOD!

NYU!

THE WEATHER IS NICE TODAY, BUT THE WAVES ARE HIGH.

HRM
よっと…

IT'S A BEAUTIFUL AUTUMN DAY.

AND TODAY, WE'RE DOING ROUTINE MAINTENANCE ON OUR GONDOLAS.

SURE THING!

AKARI, MAKE SURE YOU DRY YOUR OARS IN THE **SHADE**.

FOR GETTING OUR EQUIPMENT ALL NICE AND SPARKLING.

IT'S THE PERFECT WEATHER ...

FLAP ﾋﾟﾟ FLAP
ﾀﾀ

WHAT A GREAT VIEW!

壮観ですな。

SPLSSSH

AIKA SURE IS LATE...

ON A BEAUTIFUL DAY LIKE THIS,

I BET EVERYONE ELSE FEELS LIKE CLEANING, TOO.

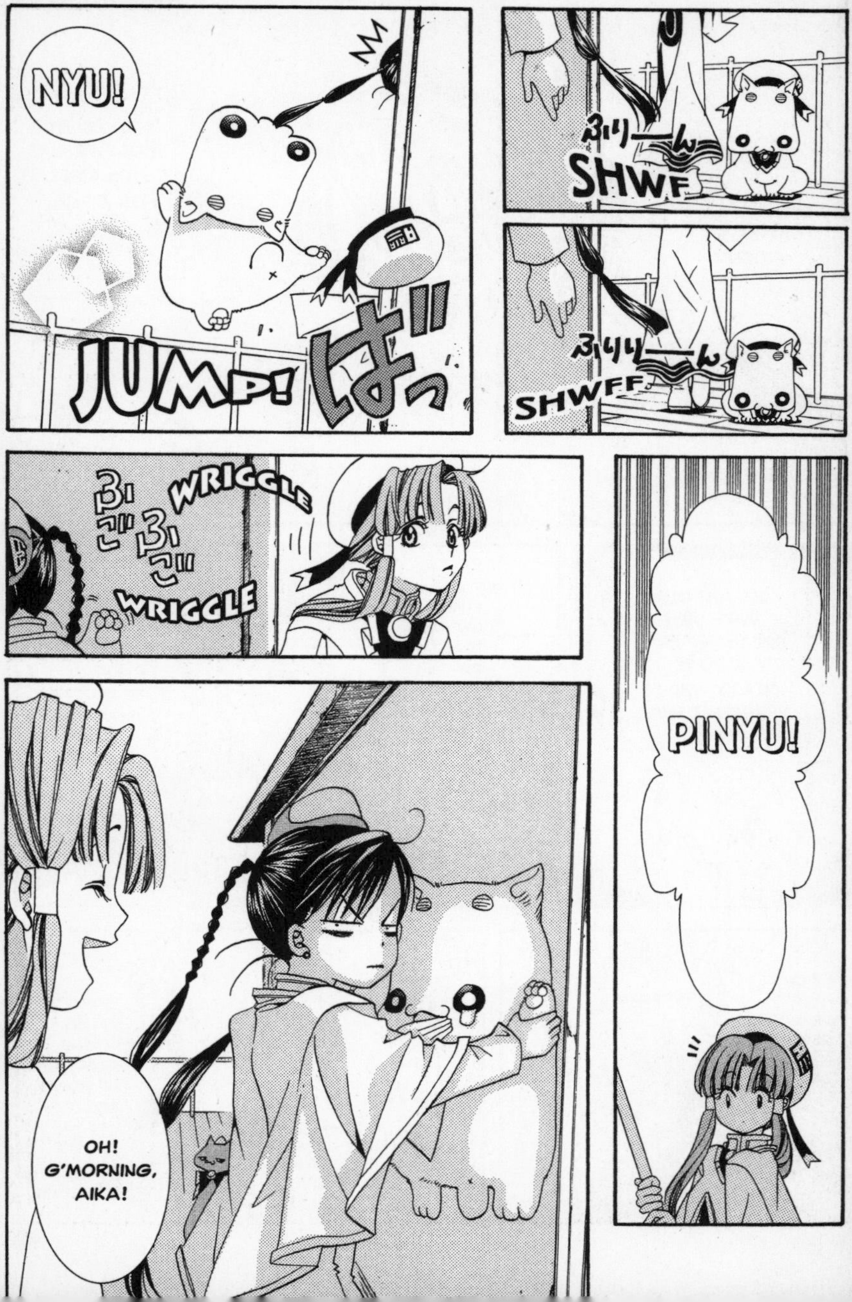
ふりーーん
SHWF
ふりりーーん
SHWFF
NYU!
JUMP!
ばっ
PINYU!
WRIGGLE
WRIGGLE
OH! G'MORNING, AIKA!

SHE'S ALSO MY **BEST** FRIEND.

AIKA IS THE FIRST FRIEND I MADE ON AQUA.

OH, AND OUR VERY OWN PRESIDENT ARIA IS JUST **CRAZY** ABOUT PRESIDENT HIME.

HMPF

SHE WORKS FOR A COMPANY CALLED HIME-YA. IT'S THE OLDEST AND MOST FAMOUS UNDINE BUSINESS IN NEO-VENEZIA.

PRESIDENT HIME ♀

SHE'S IN TRAINING TO BECOME AN UNDINE, JUST LIKE ME.

I DON'T WANT ALICIA TO SEE ME YET.

SHHHH!

HRMPH!

YOU'RE LATE. I WAS STARTING TO WORRY ABOUT Y–

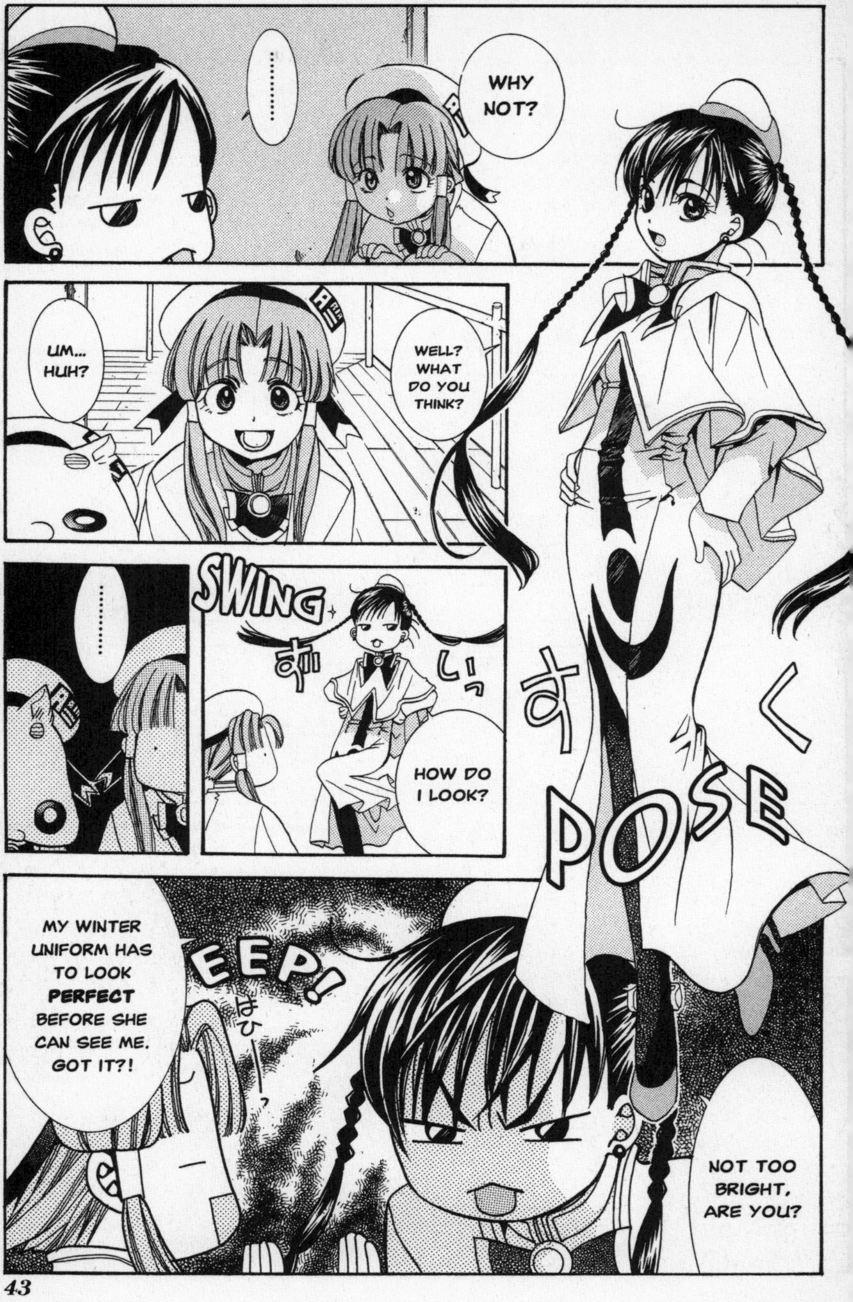
WHY NOT?
......
WELL? WHAT DO YOU THINK?
UM... HUH?
POSE
SWING
HOW DO I LOOK?
......
NOT TOO BRIGHT, ARE YOU?
MY WINTER UNIFORM HAS TO LOOK **PERFECT** BEFORE SHE CAN SEE ME. GOT IT?!
EEP!
はひー

A LOT OF PEOPLE LOOK UP TO HER...

ALICIA IS ONE OF THE MOST SKILLED UNDINES ON ALL OF AQUA.

OH! YEAH, YOU LOOK GREAT IN IT!

WELL, WELL...

AND AIKA IS ONE OF THEM.

GOOD MORNING!

AIKA. YOU'RE HERE.

OH, MY!
ゆーん

THANK YOU SOOO MUCH! ♡

ARIA COMPANY

OVERLY CUTE

THE MEW UNIFORM REALLY SUITS YOU!

WELL, LET'S GET STARTED!

HOWDY! I'M FROM UMINEKO TRANSPORT & CARRY!

THANK YOU FOR COMING.

DRYDOCKING OUR GONDOLAS.

TODAY'S MAIN EVENT:

KER-KLUNK

AND GIVE THEM A REALLY GOOD CLEANING.

THAT MEANS, WE MOVE THE GONDOLAS ONTO LAND...

ジャララララララ
CHNKCHNKCHNK

SPLOOSH

HERE GOES.

OK!

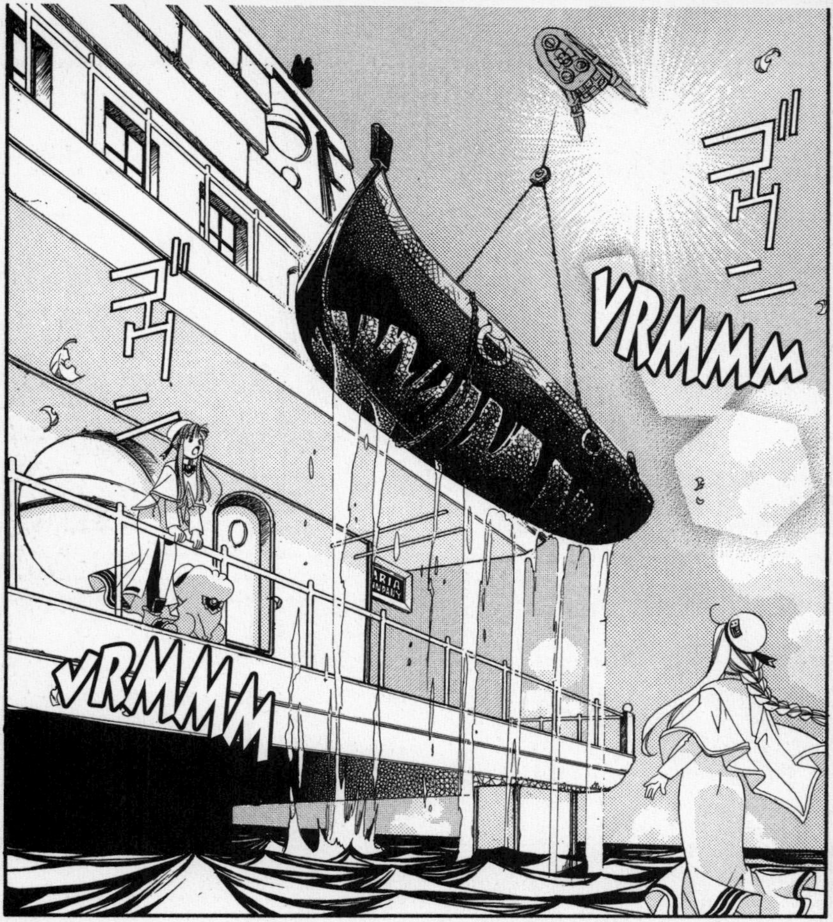
VRMMM
VRMMM

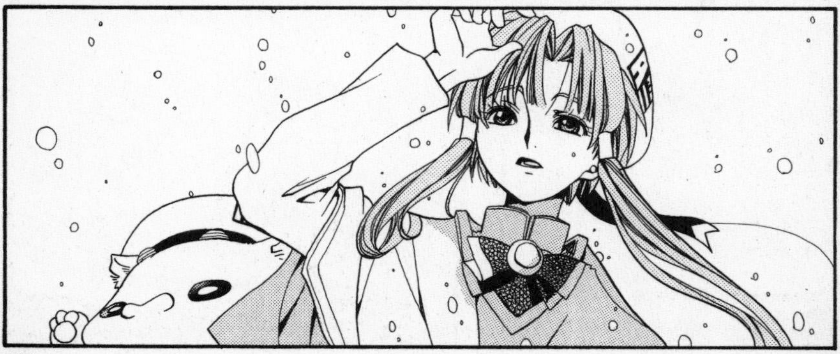

USUALLY, WE UNDINES...

ONLY SEE OUR GONDOLAS ON THE **WATER**.

VRRRR

VRRRR

OK, KEEP IT COMING.

THEY LOOK SO DIFFERENT UP IN THE AIR LIKE THAT.

KA-TUNK

VRMMM

VRMMM

I'M GOING TO THE MARITIME TRANSPORT OFFICE TO TAKE CARE OF THE RENEWALS.

OK, YOU TWO,

WHOA!

CLIP

CLIP

CLIP

CLIP

WHILE I'M GONE, I WANT YOU TO GET THOSE GONDOLAS NICE AND SHINY, OK?

SEE YOU SOON!

YES, MA'AM!

THERE'S ALL KINDS OF WEIRD **STUFF** STUCK ON THE GONDOLA.

よっと

WHOA!

PRESIDENT ARIA! ARE YOU OKAY?

DRIP

OH MY GOSH!

あわわ

だら～

AKARI!

IT LOOKS SLIMY.

べろ～ LICK!

OH!

CATCH!

WHAT'S THIS?

A SCRAPER.

EEK!

TO GET ALL THOSE **SHELLS** OFF THE GONDOLA.

CRUSTY!

ALRIGHT!

OKAY! LET'S **DO** THIS!

THIS IS FUN! ♡

AHAHAHAHAHA

SPLSSSHH

OH!

SKRK

OHH!

SKRK

PINK

PINK

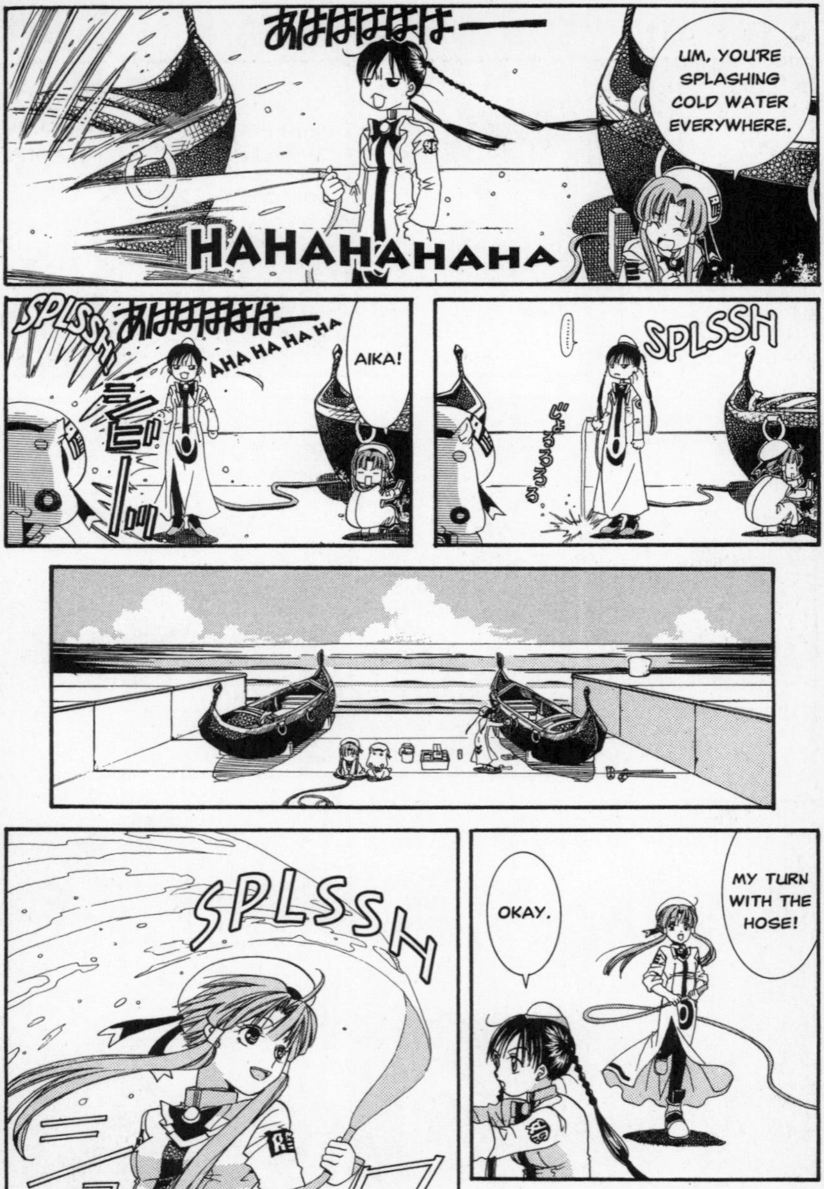
UM, YOU'RE SPLASHING COLD WATER EVERYWHERE.
あははははは—
HAHAHAHAHA
......
SPLSSH
AIKA!
SPLSSH
あははははは—
AHA HA HA HA HA
MY TURN WITH THE HOSE!
OKAY.
SPLSSH

A RAINBOW!

IT'S SO PRETTY

SPLSSSHHHH

OUCH...

SMACK

COME SEE **THIS**!

POINK!

NOW WHAT?

HEY, AIKA! AIKAAAAAA!

TWITCH

NO, NO. LOOK AT THE PUDDLE!

YEAH, THEY'RE BUBBLES. AND?!

DOESN'T IT LOOK LIKE THAT RAINBOW FROM EARLIER JUST FELL RIGHT INTO THIS WATER?

I SEE DETERGENT. BIG WHOOP.

WHA...?

YOU REALLY NEED TO CUT THIS OUT.

TA-DA!

AND THIS...

IS A SPECIAL FINISHING WAX, HANDMADE BY ALICIA!

THIS IS A WATERPROOF COAT...

TNK

TNK

THIS IS A LUBRICANT ...

NOPE! BECAUSE ...

AREN'T YOU DONE **YET**?

SLOWPOKE!

HEY!

IT'D BE A SHAME TO JUST **RUSH THROUGH** SOMETHING LIKE THIS.

SPLSSHH

I GUESS I'LL START ON THE SECOND COAT.

AND WE ARE **DONE**!

WOO-HOO!

CLAP

CLAP

CLAP

CLAP

CLAP

HMM.

GOOD.

YUP!

THEY SURE LOOK GREAT, HUH?

PINYU!

気持ちよく眠ってしまった…

PRESIDENT ARIA?

I DOZED RIGHT OFF...

AKARI!

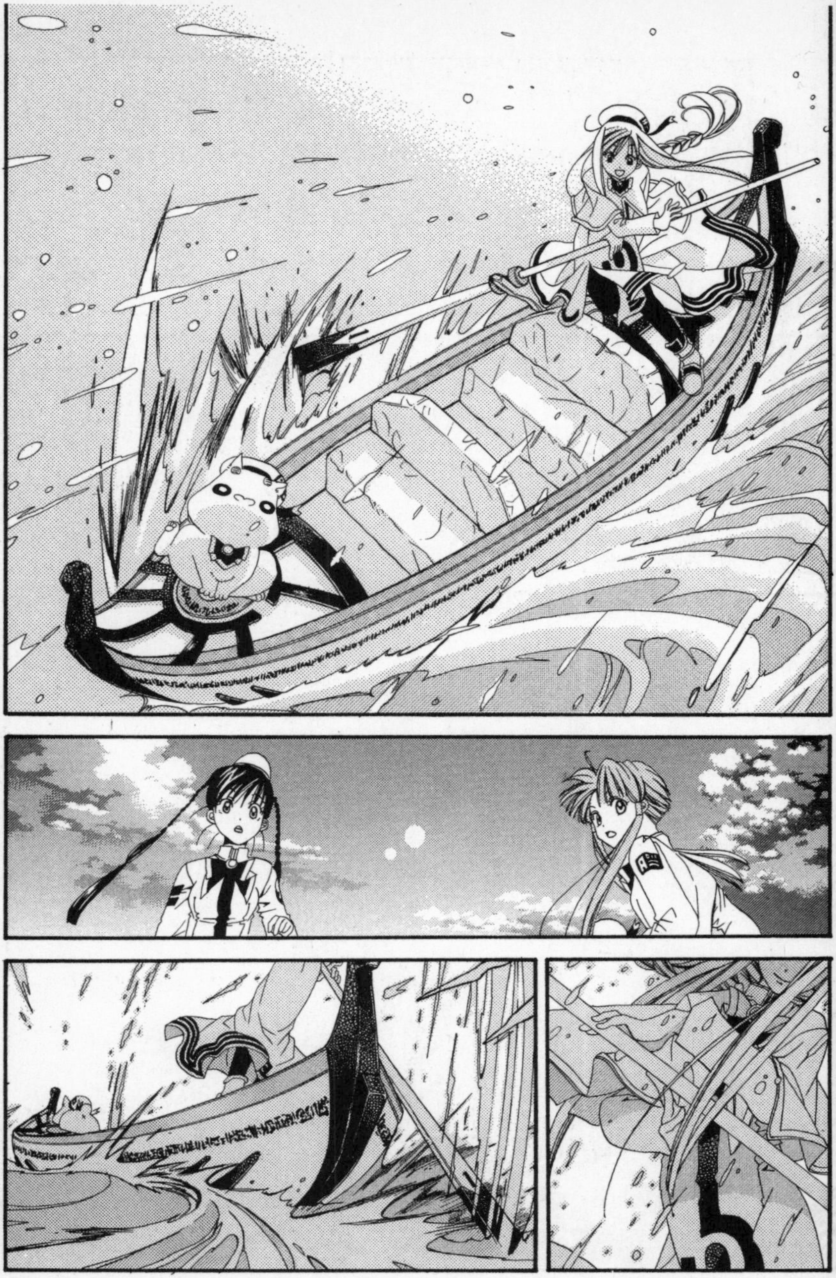

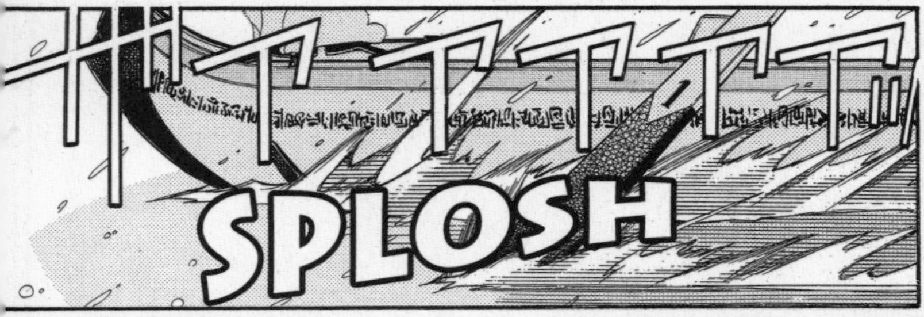
SPLOSH

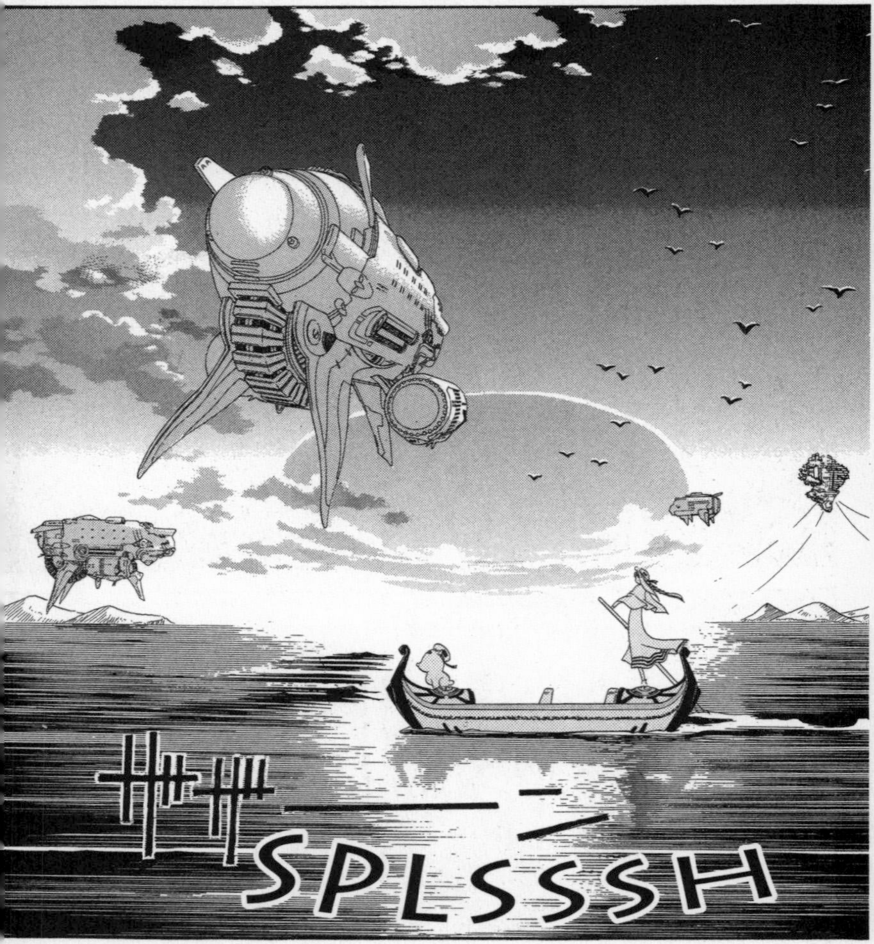
SPLSSSH

I THINK ALICIA IS THE BEST UNDINE ON AQUA!

SHE HANDLES HER SO **PERFECTLY**!

OF COURSE.

HOW PRETTY... きれい...

WHA..?

ME, TOO. ♥

GET YER OWN OPINION.

DON'T BE SILLY.

GONG

WAUGH!

ARE YOU NUTS?

I WONDER IF WE'LL EVER BE JUST LIKE HER...

OF COURSE WE WILL.

I MEAN, WE REALLY LIKE GONDOLAS, RIGHT?

YUP!

SPLSSSHH

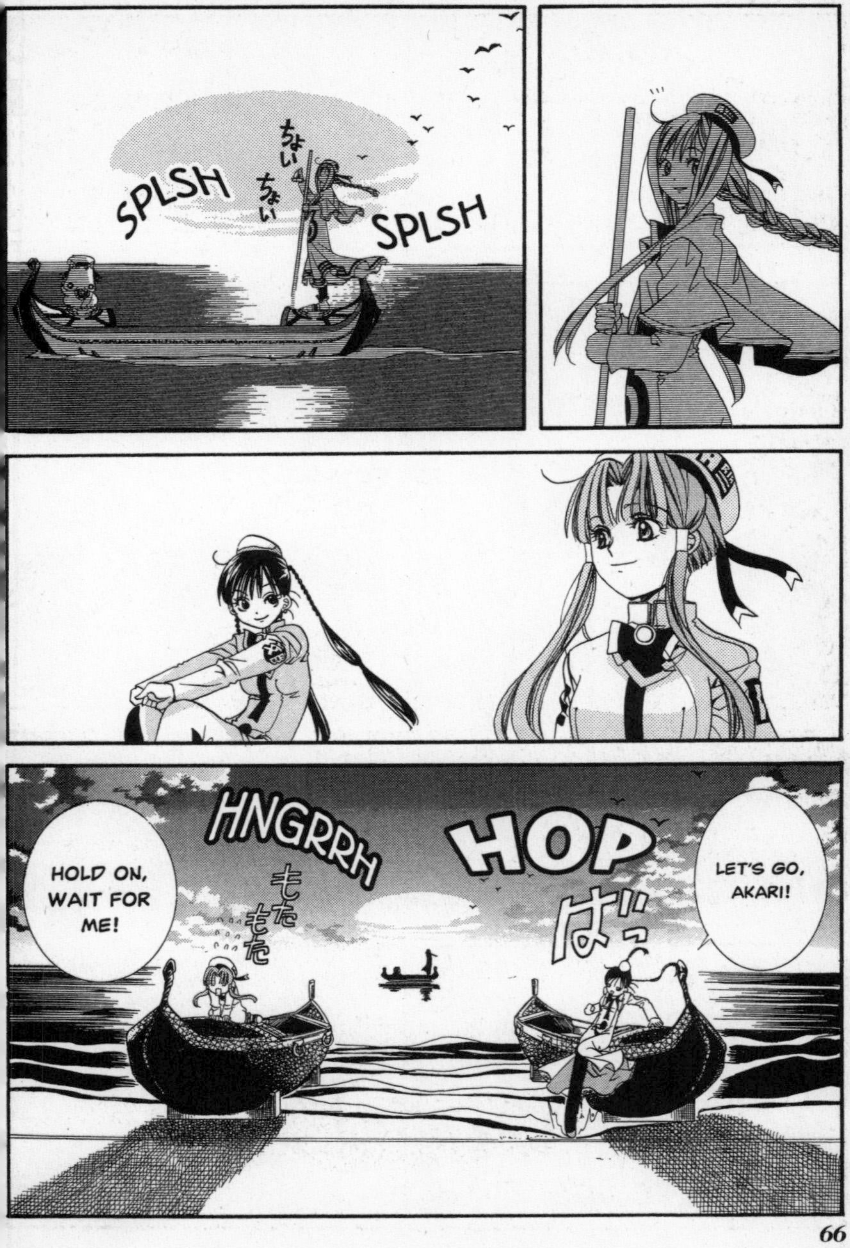
SPLSH
ちょい ちょい
SPLSH
LET'S GO, AKARI!
HOP
はっ
HNGRRH
もた もた
HOLD ON, WAIT FOR ME!

AFTER THAT, THE THREE OF US...

UNTIL SUNSET.

ROWED OUR GONDOLAS...

AS THE SETTING SUN REFLECTED ON ITS SURFACE...

THE WATER SPARKLED AND SHONE...

YUP.
ROWING IN A
SQUEAKY-CLEAN
GONDOLA IS THE
BEST FEELING IN
THE WORLD.

Navigation03 THE BRIDGE OF SIGHS

SHE'S TAKING ME TO SOME LITTLE BAKERY THAT HAS THE BEST CAKES IN TOWN!

HELLO.

I'M GOING OUT WITH MY FRIEND AIKA TODAY.

SOME SAY THAT AUTUMN IS THE SEASON FOR SPORTS, OR THE ARTS...

BUT I SAY IT'S THE TIME FOR **EATING!**

IT'S ONE OF OUR TOWN'S MOST POPULAR TOURIST ATTRACTIONS.

I'M SUPPOSED TO MEET AIKA IN FRONT OF THE BRIDGE.

IT'S VERY BUSY, AND CROWDED WITH TOURISTS ALL YEAR LONG.

THE BRIDGE IS LOCATED IN THE HEART OF NEO-VENEZIA.

BUT I CAN'T HELP GETTING EXCITED EACH TIME I SEE IT.

I PASS BY HERE ALL THE TIME,

ALRIGHT, FIVE MINUTES ♡ EARLY!

AKATSUKI!

WHAT UP?

HUH?

CAKE, CAKE

GRIP

OOOH!

SLINK

THIS IS AKATSUKI.

WHEN I STARTED WORKING AS AN UNDINE, HE WAS MY VERY FIRST CUSTOMER.

LONG TIME NO SEE, PIGTAILS.

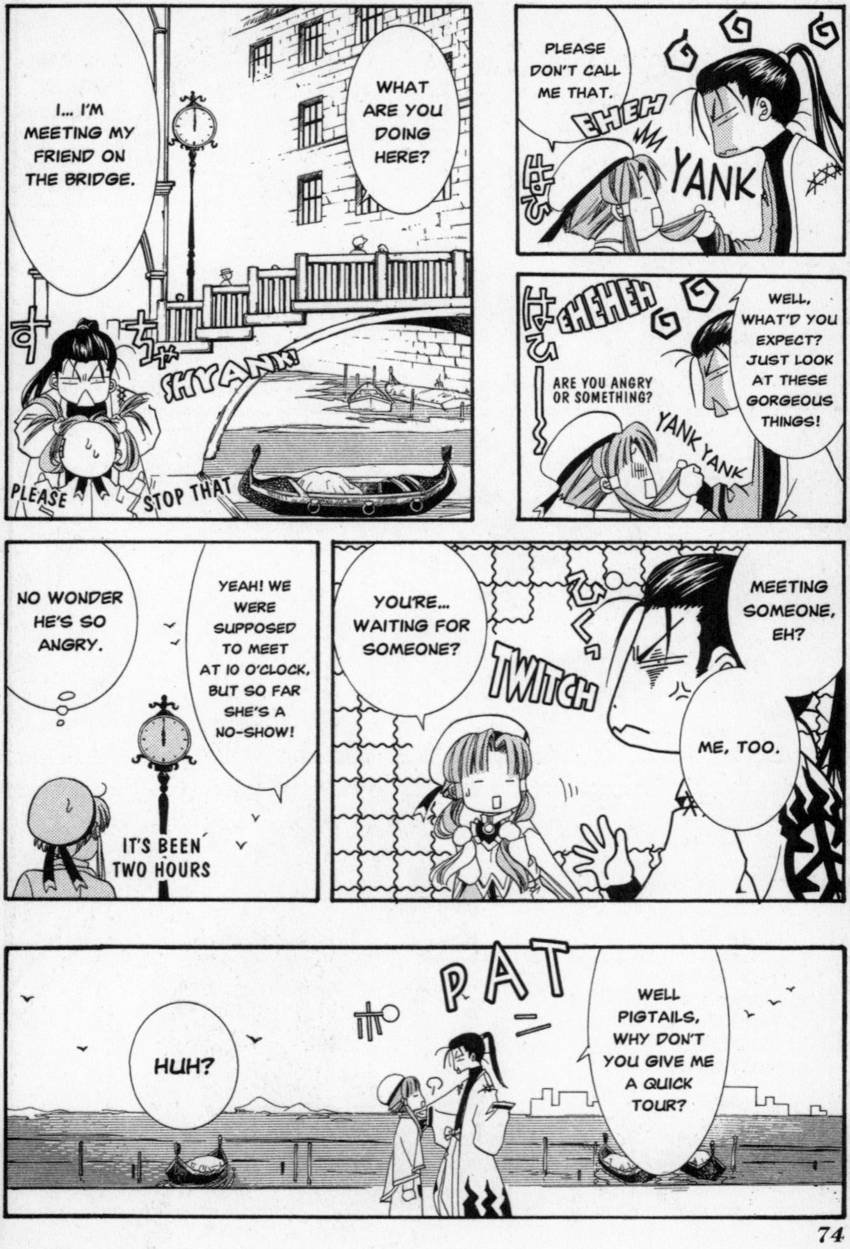
PLEASE DON'T CALL ME THAT.
EHEH
YANK
WELL, WHAT'D YOU EXPECT? JUST LOOK AT THESE GORGEOUS THINGS!
EHEHEH
ARE YOU ANGRY OR SOMETHING?
YANK YANK
WHAT ARE YOU DOING HERE?
I... I'M MEETING MY FRIEND ON THE BRIDGE.
SHYANK!
PLEASE
STOP THAT
MEETING SOMEONE, EH?
ME, TOO.
YOU'RE... WAITING FOR SOMEONE?
TWITCH
YEAH! WE WERE SUPPOSED TO MEET AT 10 O'CLOCK, BUT SO FAR SHE'S A NO-SHOW!
NO WONDER HE'S SO ANGRY.
IT'S BEEN TWO HOURS
WELL PIGTAILS, WHY DON'T YOU GIVE ME A QUICK TOUR?
PAT
HUH?

BUT YOU'RE FROM THIS TOWN!

IDIOT!

UM, WHY WOULD YOU...?

CUZ I'M SICK OF WAITING! I NEED SOMETHING TO TURN THIS MOOD OF MINE AROUND.

むん

HMPH!

I WAS BORN AND RAISED ON THE FLOATING ISLAND.

WHAT MAKES YOU THINK I KNOW THE TOWN DOWN HERE, HUH?

AKATSUKI HAS A VERY RESPECTABLE POSITION ON THE FLOATING ISLAND.

HE'S WHAT THEY CALL A "SALAMANDER," SOMEONE WHO'S JOB IS TO CONTROL THE WEATHER.

BUT INSIDE HE'S REALLY A NICE PERSON. MAYBE.

I'M NOT "PIGTAILS."

YOU UNDERSTAND, RIGHT PIGTAILS?

HE CAN BE A LITTLE SCARY...

SPLSSSH

BUT I'M STILL IN TRAINING. I'M NOT ALLOWED TO GIVE TOURS WITHOUT AN INSTRUCTOR PRESENT...

BUT I'M WAITING FOR SOMEONE...

LOOK, WE'LL STAY WITHIN SIGHT OF THE BRIDGE. THAT WAY, THERE'LL BE NO PROBLEM. RIGHT?

RRRR

BUT I'M NOT A CUSTOMER.

CLING

HUH?

HOP

THERE WE GO

SO I CAN'T... AKATSUKI!

HE... WANTS TO GET A FREE TOUR OUT OF THIS.

GONG

ご～ん

SCAMPER

WE'RE FRIENDS, RIGHT?

FINE.

FINE. BUT JUST FOR A LITTLE WHILE.

IF YOU'LL PLEASE LOOK OVER TO YOUR RIGHT...

営業 **BUSINESS**

スマイル **SMILE**

MAY I HAVE YOUR ATTENTION?

YOU'LL SEE THE MARCO POLO INTERNATIONAL SPACEPORT.

IT'S THE "GATEWAY" INTO TOWN FOR ALL AERIAL CRAFT.

WOAH, THAT'S HUGE!

YOU SOUND LIKE YOU KNOW WHAT YOU'RE TALKING ABOUT, PIGTAILS.

WELL, I AM STUDYING.

THE BUILDING WAS ORIGINALLY A PALACE FOR THE IMMIGRANT GOVERNORS...

WHO OVERSAW COLONIZATION DURING THE "MARS MIGRATION PROJECT" 150 YEARS AGO.

ARIA 1

ON YOUR RIGHT, YOU CAN SEE SAINT MARK'S BASILICA,

THE CLOCK TOWER AND THE BELL TOWER.

NEXT IS SAN MARCO SQUARE.

MARS.

THE COOL-LOOKING THING ON TOP OF THE PILLAR!

OH, THAT.

HEY, PIGTAILS! WHAT'S THAT?

HM?

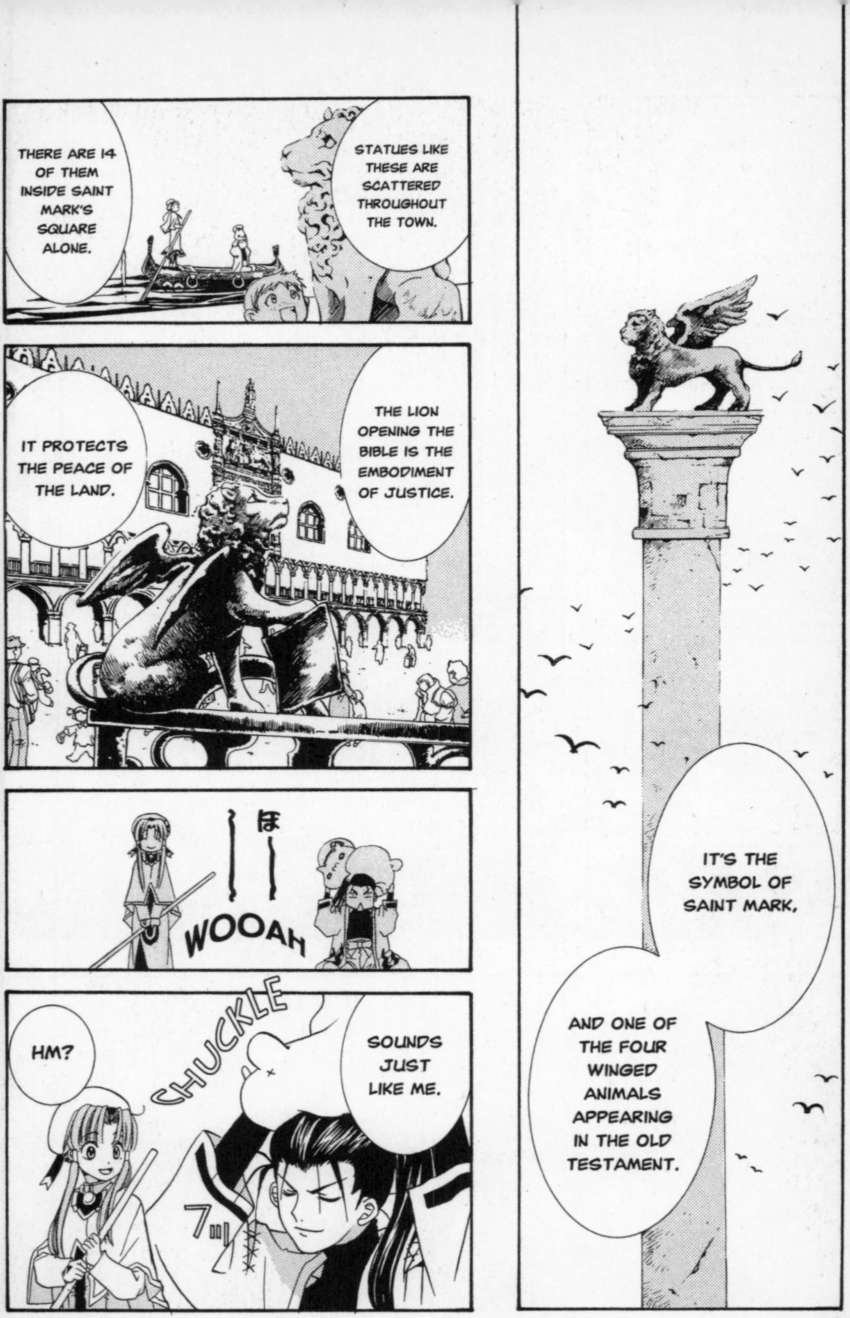
IT'S THE SYMBOL OF SAINT MARK,
AND ONE OF THE FOUR WINGED ANIMALS APPEARING IN THE OLD TESTAMENT.
STATUES LIKE THESE ARE SCATTERED THROUGHOUT THE TOWN.
THERE ARE 14 OF THEM INSIDE SAINT MARK'S SQUARE ALONE.
THE LION OPENING THE BIBLE IS THE EMBODIMENT OF JUSTICE.
IT PROTECTS THE PEACE OF THE LAND.
ほー
WOOAH
SOUNDS JUST LIKE ME.
CHUCKLE
フッ
HM?

ARIA 1

THE FLOATING ISLANDS WERE MADE TO REGULATE THE WEATHER, AND **SCORES** OF THEM ARE SITUATED THROUGHOUT THE ATMOSPHERE.

THE SUN

FLOATING ISLAND

MAN HOME (EARTH)

ILLUSTRATED BY AKATSUKI

AQUA

AQUA IS MUCH FURTHER FROM THE SUN THAN MAN HOME...

THE PEOPLE HERE HAVE AN IDEAL LIVING ENVIRONMENT.

EVERY DAY, SALAMANDERS WORK HARD TO ENSURE THAT...

AS A SALAMANDER, MY JOB...

AKATSUKI! PLEASE SIT DOWN!

WOBBLE WOBBLE

WE ARE THE EMBODIMENT OF JUSTICE.

THAT'S RIGHT!

IN OTHER WORDS, IT IS **WE** WHO PROTECT THE PEACE OF THESE LANDS!

IS TO CONTROL THE LIGHT AND ENERGY OF THE FLOATING ISLAND. THOUGH I'M STILL IN TRAINING...

IT'S ONE O'CLOCK ALREADY?

WE SHOULD GET BACK TO THE BRIDGE.

SPLSSSHH

··········

コ゛ ゛

DING

DONG

YEAH!

AND YOU SEEM TO BE IN A BETTER MOOD.

I'M SURE MY FRIEND IS HERE NOW.

ヒュル ル ·········· ル ル

NO-SHOW.

WHOOOOOO

AND THEN I CAN'T REMEMBER WHAT I WAS THINKING ABOUT. DOES THAT HAPPEN TO YOU?

WHEN I'M WAITING FOR SOMEONE, SOMETIMES MY MIND JUST DRIFTS...

I'VE BEEN HERE FOR **THREE FREAKIN' HOURS** ALREADY.

AIKA SURE IS LATE.

SPACED OUT

I WOULDN'T.

I KIND OF LIKE WHEN THAT HAPPENS.

ENOUGH!

AKATSUKI! YOU'LL BE MORE RELAXED IF YOU SIT UP AGAINST THE WALL.

HEEEY!

IMPATIENT

CLICK

CLICK

HOP INCREASINGLY IMPATIENT

SPACED OUT

GLARE

GEEZ

THWUMP

YOU **DO** REALIZE THAT **YOUR** FRIEND HASN'T SHOWN UP EITHER, RIGHT?

NOTHING BOTHERS YOU, DOES IT?

SCRATCH

SCRATCH

I GUESS THAT MEANS **WE'RE** ALL ANIMALS, TOO.

DID YOU KNOW THAT ANIMALS TEND TO FEEL UNEASY WHEN THERE'S SOMETHING BEHIND THEM?

REALLY. YOU DON'T SAY.

THIS IS HOPELESS.

WELL, I AM KINDA HUNGRY...

AT TIMES LIKE THESE, THE BEST WAY TO KILL TIME IS TO PEOPLE-WATCH!

PING

IT'S ALMOST THREE O'CLOCK. AREN'T YOU GETTING IMPATIENT YET?

POINT

FOR EXAMPLE, LOOK AT THAT GUY OVER THERE.

PLOP
よっこいせっと

WADDLE
ふる
ふる
WADDLE

WADDLE
ふる
ふる
WADDLE

CAN HE EVEN **GET** TO WHERE HE'S GOING BEFORE THE DAY'S OVER?

WORRY!

TUG

HE WAS WALKING SO SLOWLY.

I WONDER WHERE HE'S GOING?

TWITCH

↑ A CART USED FOR TAKING BREAKS.

NOW LISTEN HERE, PIGTAILS...

SIIIIIGH

YOU KNOW, I COULDN'T CARE LESS!

BUT HAIR-PULLING IS PROHIBITED.

SIIIGH

OH, OKAY.

YOU JUST SIGHED IN FRONT OF THE BRIDGE OF SIGHS.

HEH.

OH,

WHAT'S SO FUNNY?

YEAH. IT'S THE BRIDGE RIGHT IN FRONT OF US.

BRIDGE OF SIGHS? **THAT'S** A STRANGE NAME.

SO MANY PEOPLE HAVE SIGHED ON THAT BRIDGE OVER THE YEARS...

TUG
TUG
ちょい
ちょい

AKATSUKI! LOOK!

IT LOOKS LIKE AN ORDINARY BRIDGE TO ME.

WHY WOULD IT MAKE PEOPLE SIGH?

QUACK
ぐぁっ

QUACK
ぐぁっ

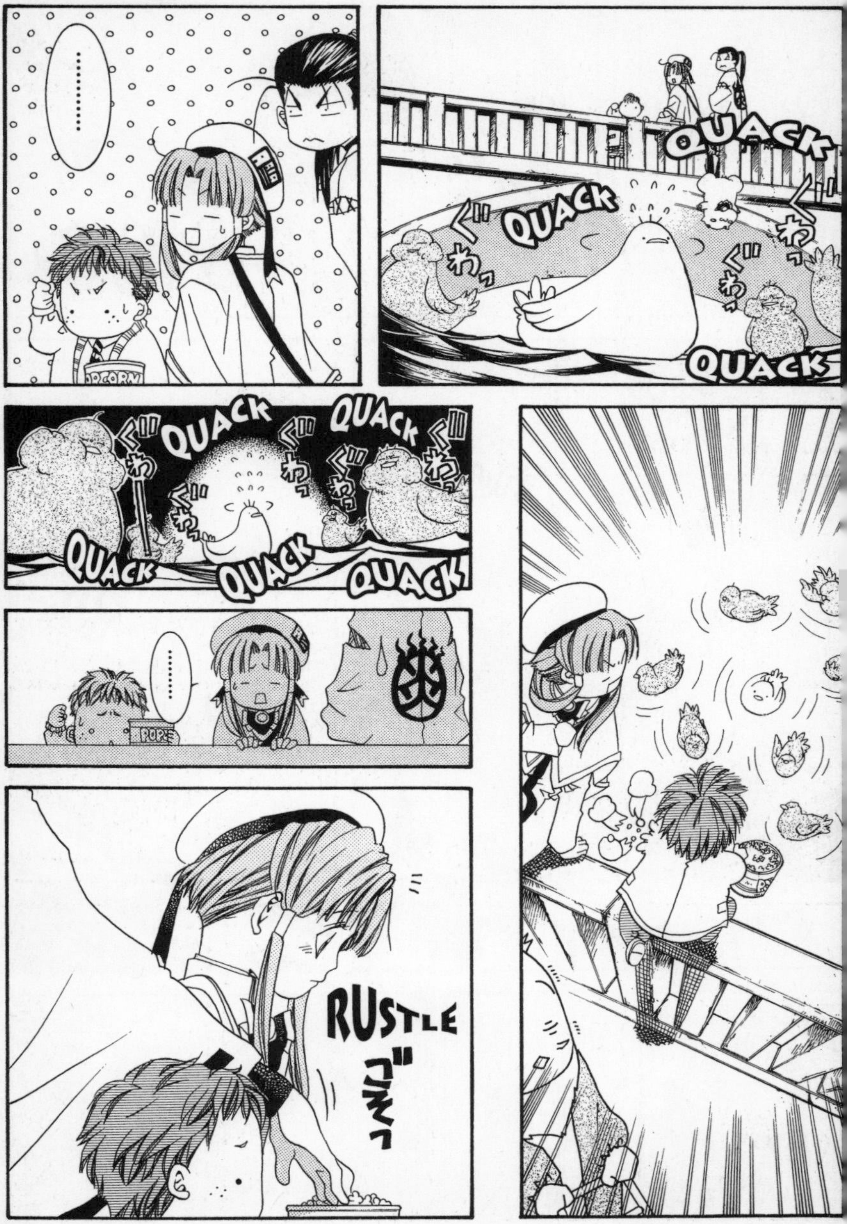
QUACK
ぐわっ
QUACK
ぐわっ
ぐわっ
QUACK
……
QUACK
ぐわっ
QUACK
ぐわっ
ぐわっ
QUACK
QUACK
QUACK
……
RUSTLE
ゴソッ

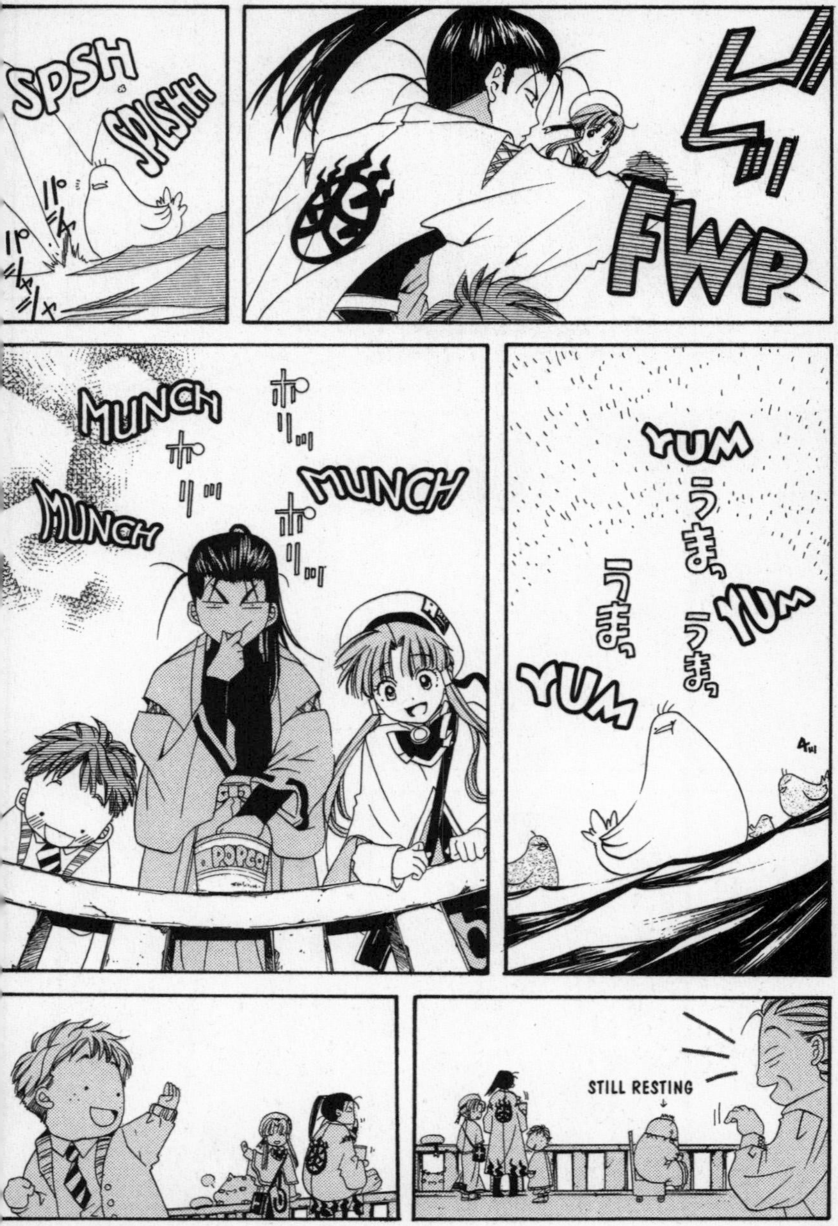
FWP
SPSH
SPLSHH
YUM
うまっ
YUM
うまっ
うまっ
YUM
MUNCH
MUNCH
MUNCH
STILL RESTING

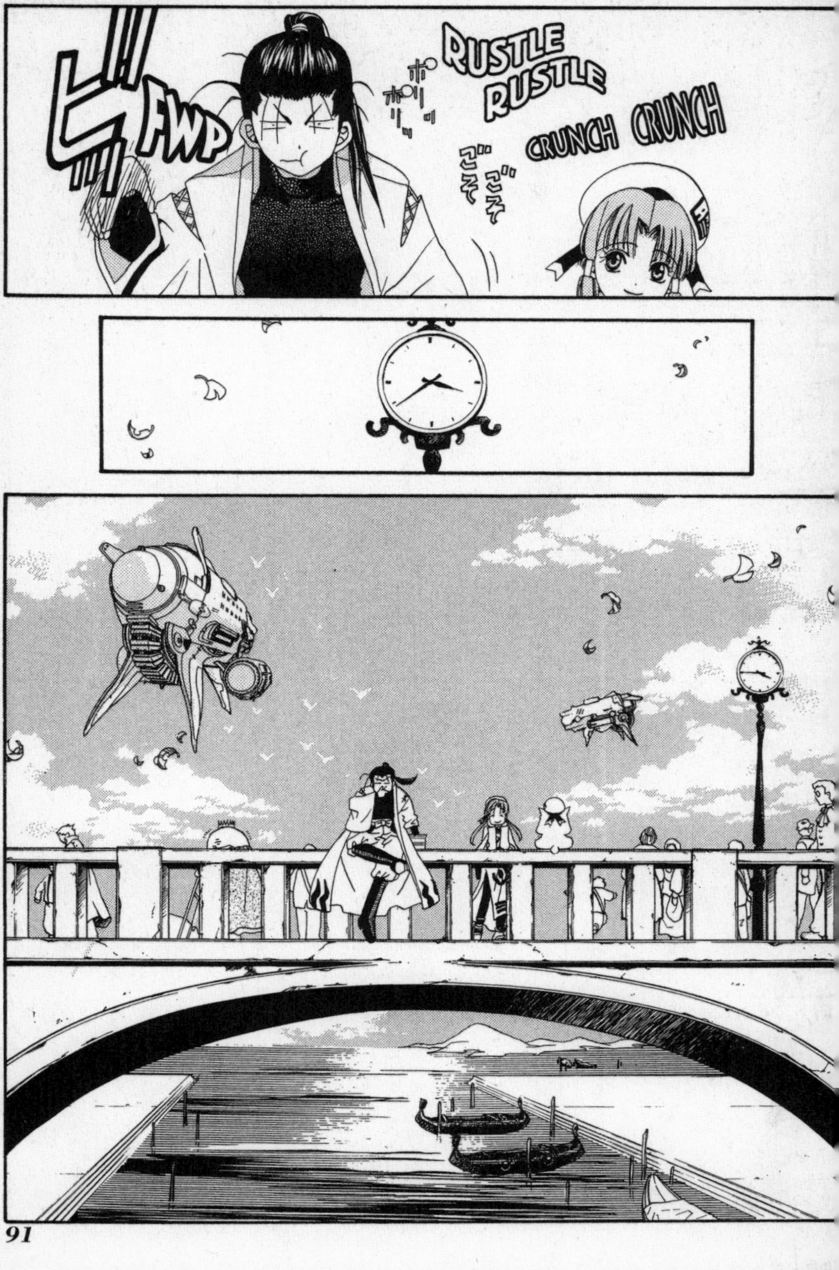
FWP
RUSTLE RUSTLE
CRUNCH CRUNCH
ごそ ごそ

DONG DONG DONG

HRARR!

AKATSUKI, IT'S FOUR O'CLOCK.

I'VE BEEN WAITING FOR **SIX HOURS** NOW

SIIIGH

AND DIDN'T EVEN REALIZE IT.

YES.

ARE YOU SERIOUS, PIGTAILS?

AND MY NAME'S NOT PIGTAILS!

A LOT OF THE BUILDINGS HERE ARE BASED ON ONES IN **OLD VENEZIA**, ON MAN HOME.

AND THERE ARE A LOT OF OLD STORIES THAT COME FROM THERE, TOO.

HEY, YOU NEVER ANSWERED ME EARLIER.

WHY WOULD PEOPLE SIGH ON THIS BRIDGE?

AND THE ONE ON THE LEFT WAS A COURTHOUSE.

THAT BUILDING ON THE RIGHT WAS A PRISON...

IN OLD VENEZIA,

LONG AGO, AFTER THE PRISONERS RECEIVED THEIR SENTENCES,

THEY'D CROSS THE BRIDGE TO THE PRISON.

I SEE

EPUU!

THEY SAY THAT EVERY PRISONER STOPPED AT LEAST ONCE WHEN THEY WERE CROSSING THE BRIDGE,

LOOKED DOWN AT THE BEAUTIFUL TOWN BELOW...

AND SIGHED IN GRIEF.

FROM ONE OF THOSE SMALL WINDOWS UP THERE...

GET TO SPEND OUR TIME IN A BEAUTIFUL PLACE LIKE THIS...

AND NOW WE...

YES.

AAH. SO THAT'S WHY PEOPLE CALL IT THE BRIDGE OF SIGHS.

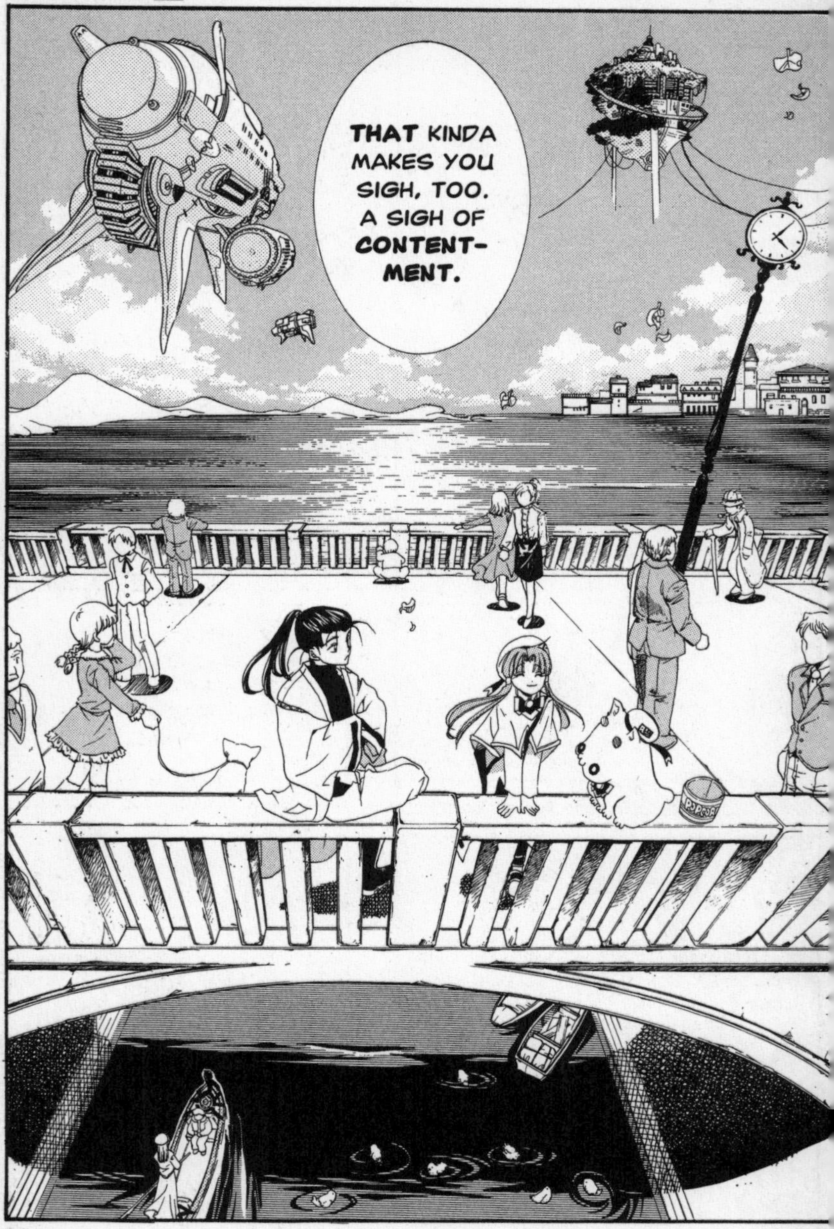
THAT KINDA MAKES YOU SIGH, TOO. A SIGH OF CONTENT-MENT.

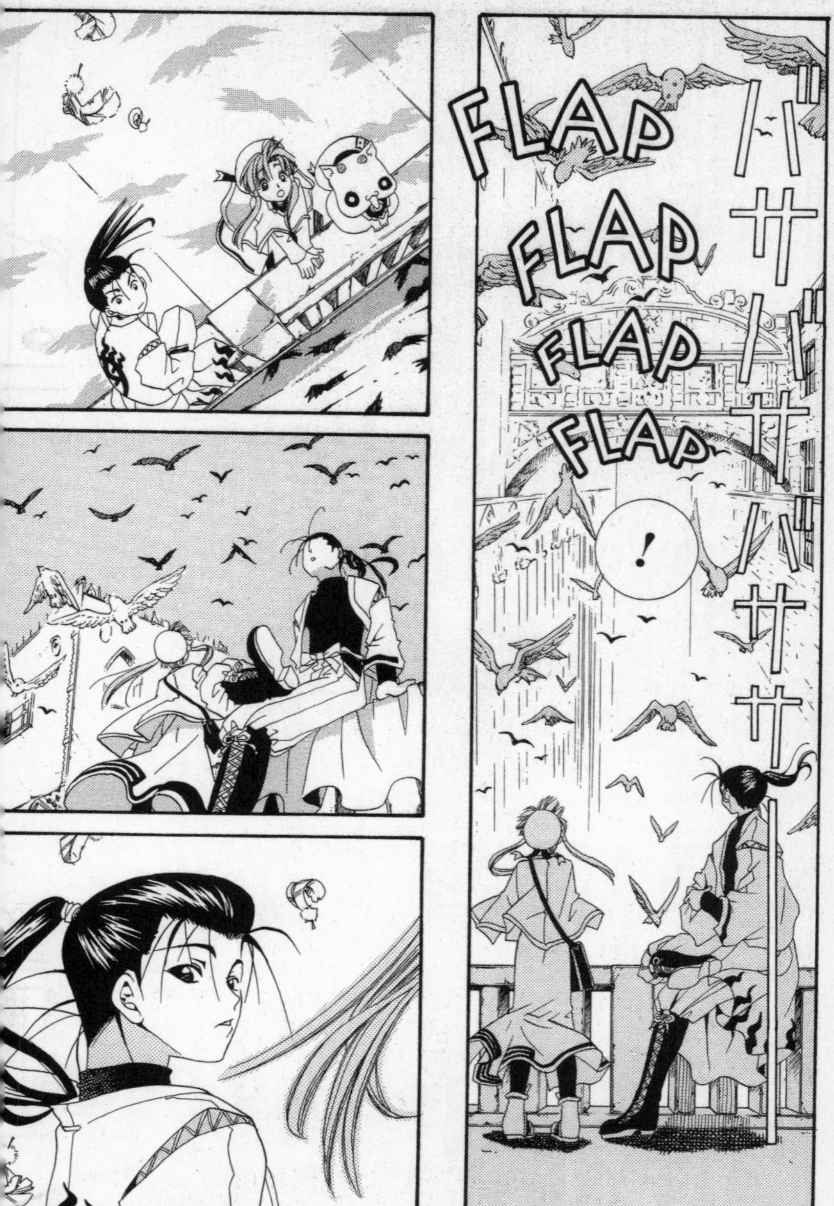

FLAP
FLAP
FLAP
FLAP
バサバサバサ
!

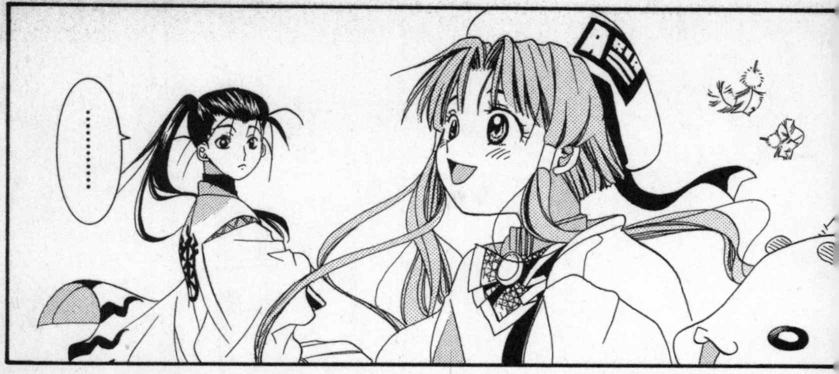
....

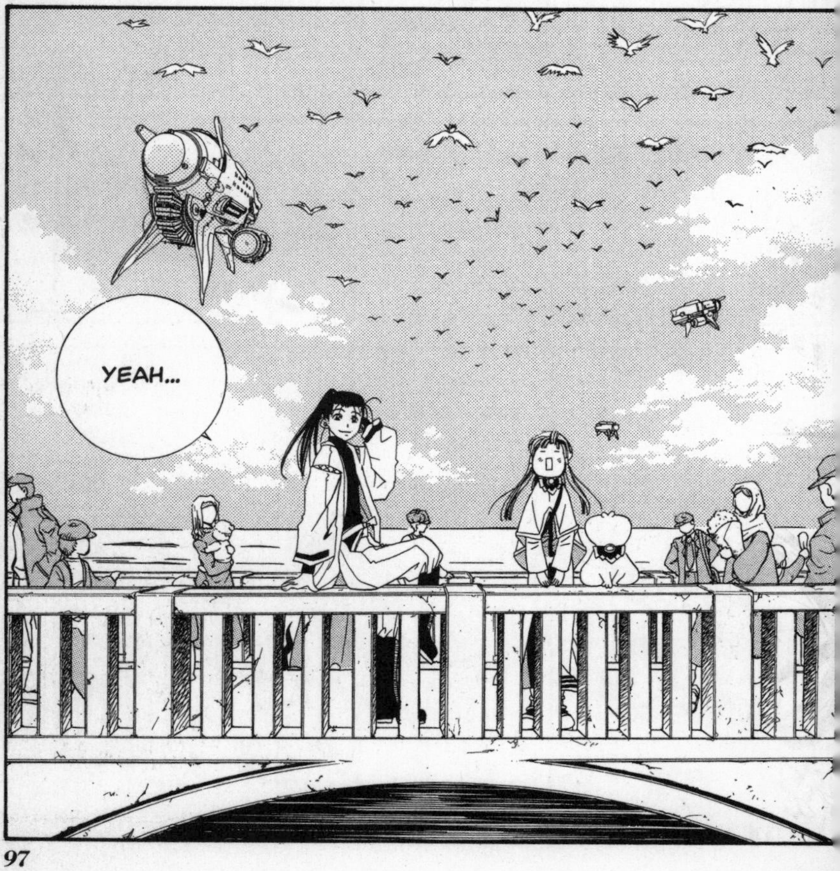
YEAH...

THWACK

!

YOU TRYIN' TO ACT COOL, OR WHAT?! FOOL!

YOU SON OF A...!

KONK!!

SORRY I'M LATE. BWEHEHEH!

OWW...

I CAN'T BELIEVE MR. SHORT-TEMPERED HERE WAITED FOR ME FOR **SIX** HOURS!

NOOGIE NOOGIE

TH... THIS MAN IS AKATSUKI'S OLDER BROTHER?

WAHAHA! LOOKS LIKE YOU'RE DOIN' JUST FINE, LITTLE BRO.

WELL, I JUST, IT'S...

GRRRGH

MUST'VE BEEN A PAIN.

WHA, UM...

I WAS WAITING FOR SOMEONE, TOO...

YOU'VE BEEN KEEPIN' HIM COMPANY ALL THIS TIME?

FLINCH

YO, MISSY!

Y... YES SIR?

A PRETTY WONDERFUL UNDINE,

EVEN ON THE GROUND.

I GUESS YOU'RE ...

FINALLY FOUND WHO HE WAS WAITING FOR.

AND THAT'S HOW AKATSUKI...

I'VE DONE A LOT OF WAITING TODAY.

IT SEEMS LIKE...

I WONDER WHAT HAPPENED.

AIKA NEVER DID SHOW UP.

SPLSSSHH

I WASN'T BORED AT ALL.

BUT...

BECAUSE THE PLACE I LIVE IN...

IS NEO-VENEZIA.

A TOWN
SO BEAUTIFUL,
IT'D MAKE
YOU SIGH.

TODAY, WE'RE GOING TO VISIT A SMALL ISLAND THAT'S FAMOUS FOR ...

HELLO. WE'RE NOW IN THE MIDDLE OF AUTUMN.

THE BEAUTIFUL AUTUMN COLORS OF ITS TREES.

NEO-VENEZIA IS LOCATED IN THE ADRIATIC SEA,

WHICH IS FAMOUS ...

FOR ITS MANY DIFFERENT ISLANDS.

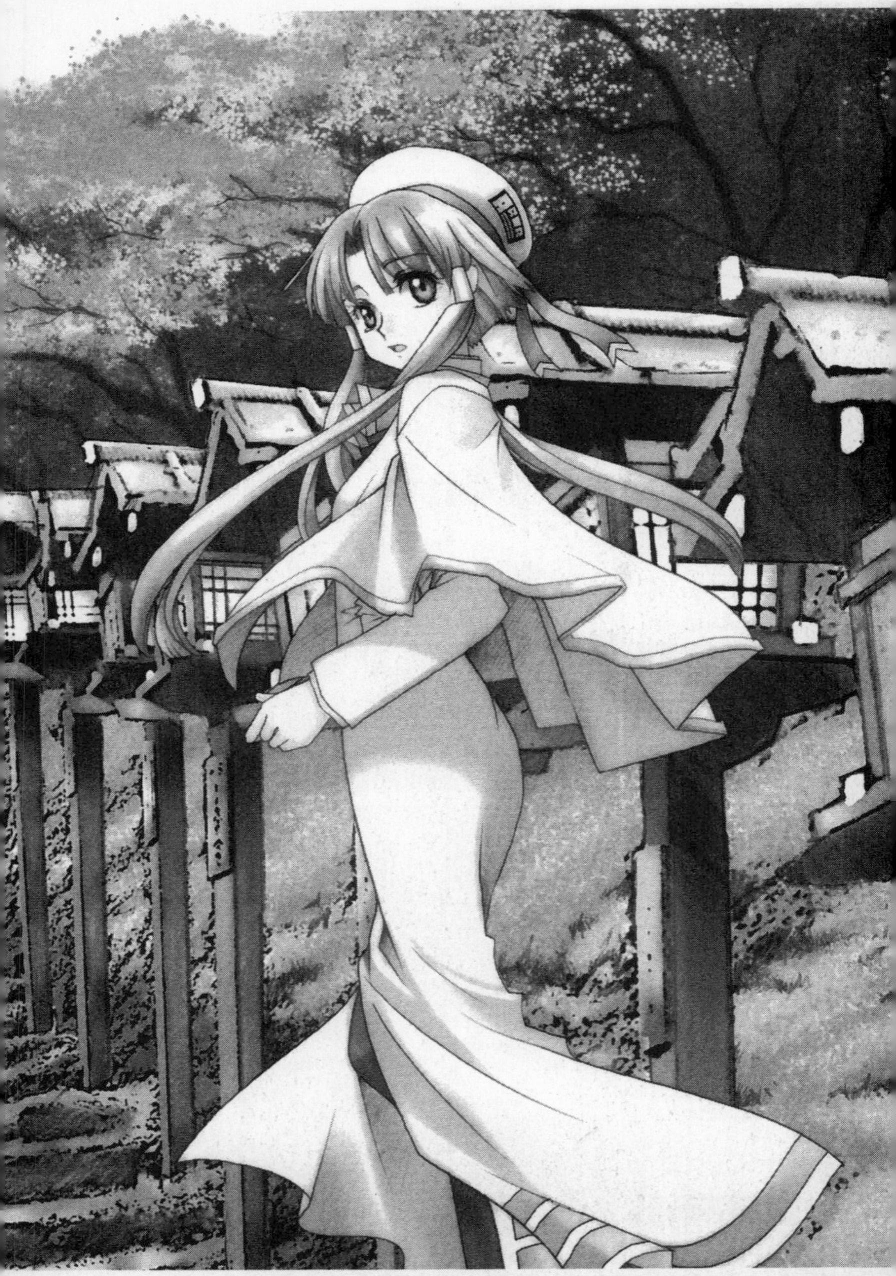

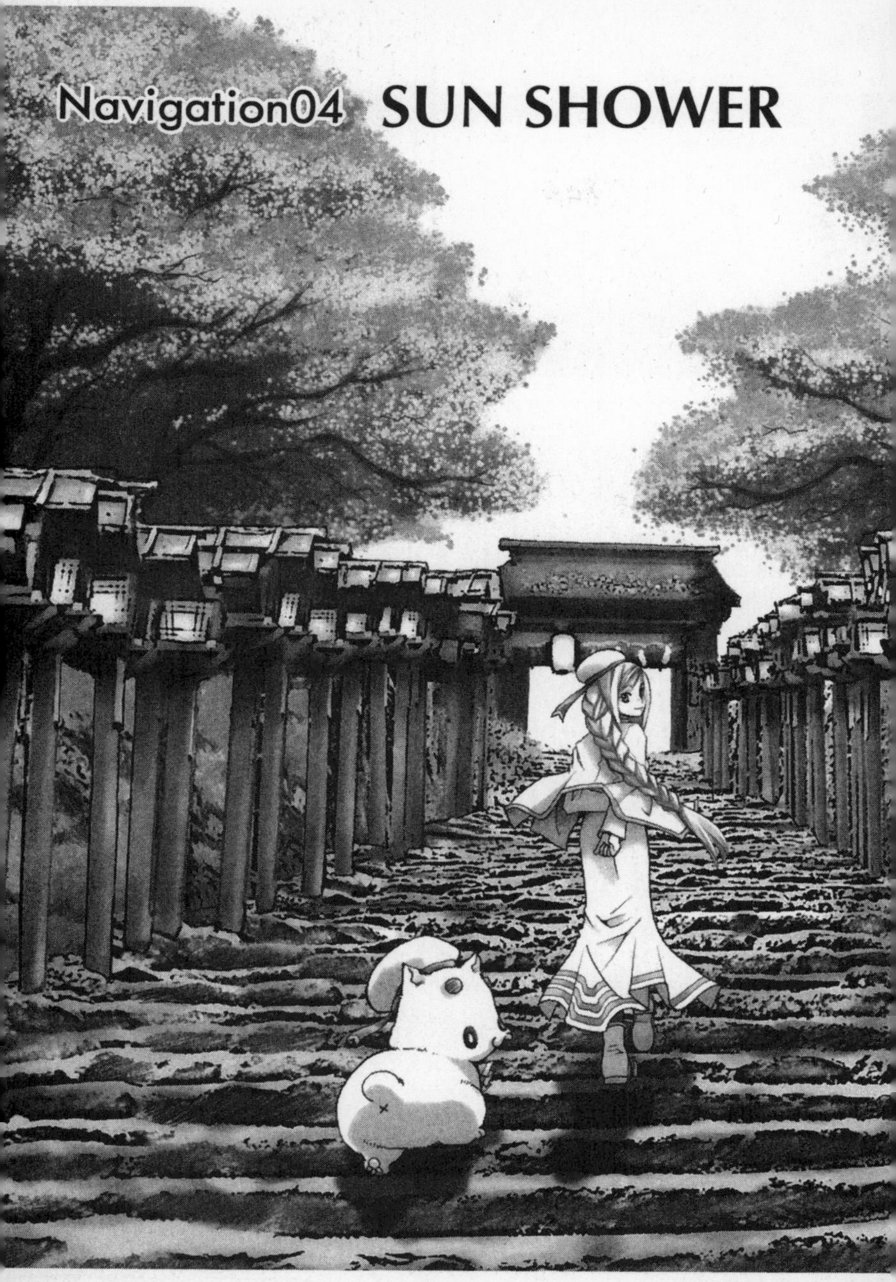
Navigation04 SUN SHOWER

PLACED ON DIFFERENT ISLANDS ACCORDING TO THEIR HOME COUNTRIES, AND BUILT VILLAGES REPRESENTATIVE OF THEIR NATIVE CULTURES.

WHEN PEOPLE FIRST COLONIZED AQUA, THEY WERE...

STILL RETAINS THE **FEEL** OF THOSE OLD COUNTRIES.

TODAY, EACH OF THE ISLANDS ...

WOW!

LOOK AT ALL THE BIG SHRINE GATES!

I'VE ONLY SEEN SHRINES LIKE THIS IN OLD DOCUMENTARIES!

THIS IS AMAZING!

IT SAYS THAT THIS ISLAND USED TO REPRESENT JAPAN.

WOW!

OH, THAT'S AN INARI FOX.

HE'S THE **GUARDIAN** OF THIS SHRINE.

WOW...

UM, WHAT'S THIS?

FWP

WHAT A STRANGE FACE...

WAFT

WAFT

WELCOME.

TEA

WE SHOULD GET SOME!

SHWP!

ALRIGHT!

INARIZUSHI!

IT SAYS THAT THIS SHOP HAS SOME DELICIOUS INARIZUSHI!

GUIDE

GUIDE

YES, MA'AM.

DID YOU TWO COME TO SEE THE AUTUMN LEAVES?

TO GO.

TEN INARIZUSHI, PLEASE.

THANK YOU.

YOU MIGHT RUN INTO AN **INARI FOX.**

ON A BEAUTIFUL DAY LIKE THIS,

OH BOY!

I WANNA SEE HIM! I WANNA SEE HIM!

SHAKE SHAKE SHAKE

HA HA HA

HE SOMETIMES SHOWS UP HERE, IN THE **HUMAN** WORLD.

THE INARI FOX OF THIS SHRINE IS QUITE MISCHIEVOUS.

ZOOM

WHAT? YOU CAN ACTUALLY **SEE** ONE?

OH DEAR

YES, IF YOU'RE LUCKY.

110

HE DECIDES TO TAKE SOMEONE **WITH** HIM.

EVERY NOW AND THEN...

BUT YOU MUST BE CAREFUL.

ONCE HE TAKES YOU...

THE SPIRIT WORLD AND HUMAN WORLD ARE VERY DIFFERENT.

YOU CAN NEVER RETURN HERE AGAIN!

TEA

THANK YOU!

JUST RELAX AND ENJOY THE SCENERY.

HA HA HA HA

YOU'RE KIDDING, RIGHT?

MY, MY!

ALRIGHT, THEN. LET'S GO!!

YEE-HA!

FSSHHH

OH MY GOODNESS!

EVERYTHING IS BRIGHT RED!

IT'S LIKE SOMEONE CAST A SPELL TO TURN EVERYTHING RED!

MY, MY!

あら あら

AMAZING...

113

IT'S SO PRETTY....

RUSTLE

RUSTLE

FWSHHHHH

THAT IT'S ALMOST **FRIGHTENING.**

AKARI?
AKARI!

HUH?

SORRY.

· · · · · · ·

DON'T GET
LOST, OKAY?

WHAT?

I THOUGHT I SAW SOMEONE.

WHAT'S THE MATTER?

HOW UNUSUAL.

DRIP

IT RAINS EVEN WHEN THE SUN'S OUT?!

YOU'VE NEVER SEEN ONE BEFORE?

OH YEAH, THE WEATHER ON YOUR HOMEWORLD IS COMPLETELY AUTOMATED, ISN'T IT?

A "SUN SHOWER."

FWSSHH...

IT'S A SUN SHOWER!

IT'S AMAZING! ♥

THERE WAS **ANOTHER** NAME FOR SUN SHOWERS. A PRETTY ONE...

WHAT WAS IT AGAIN?

YOU KNOW, I REMEMBER LONG AGO...

OKAY.

LET'S FIND SOME COVER.

....

SHHHAAAA

PHEW!

HUFF HUFF

THP·THP·THP

ALICIA?

HUH?

BUT WE WERE HOLDING HANDS!

SHOCK

AM I... LOST?

IT'S ONLY SPRINKLING NOW, SO WE SHOULD BE OKAY.

HOP

NYU

PRESIDENT ARIA!

WHY DON'T WE GO LOOK FOR ALICIA?

....

SHHHAAAA

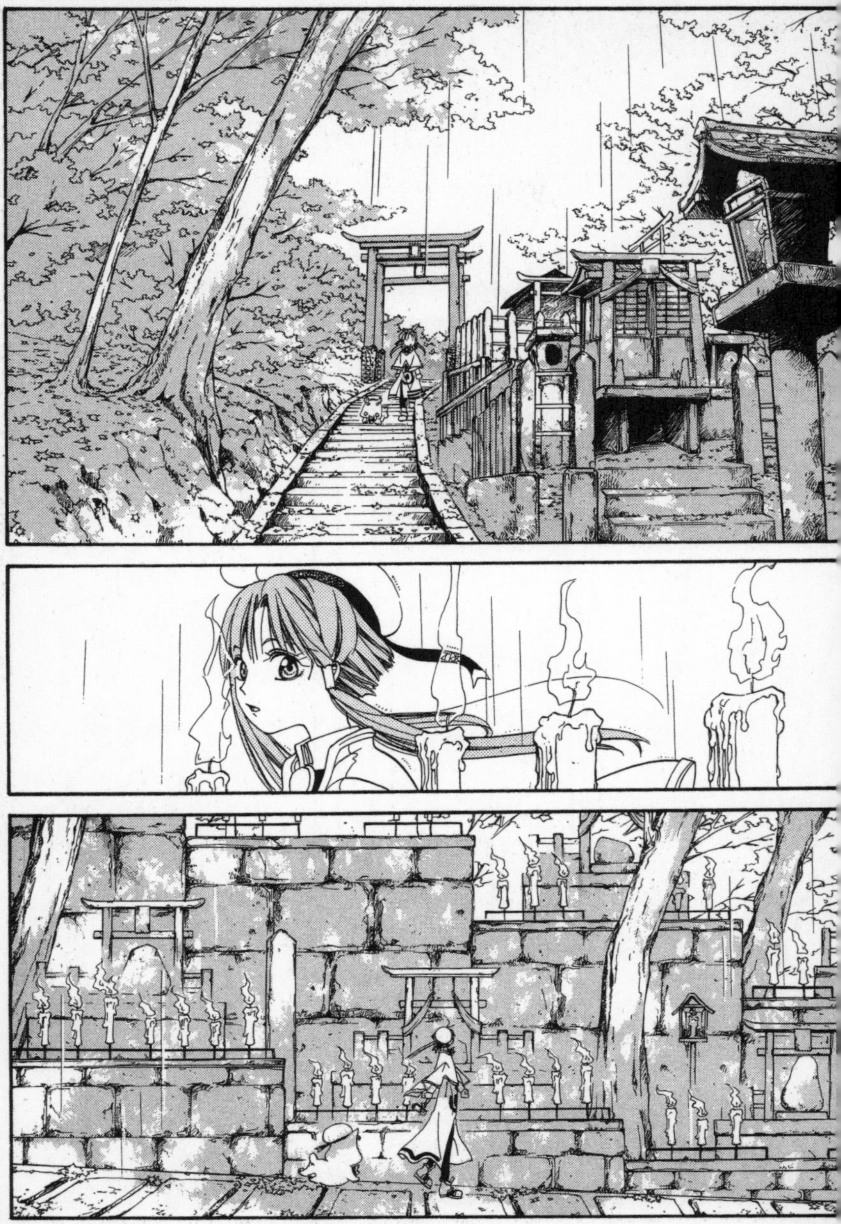

PRESIDENT ARIA!

IT LEADS TO A DIFFERENT **WORLD** OR SOMETHING.

THIS PATH LOOKS ALMOST LIKE...

SKT

WHAT AM I TALKING ABOUT?

OH!

OKAY, DON'T PANIC.

THUMP THUMP

MY IMAGINATION?

WAS IT JUST...

SOMETHING HAS BEEN FOLLOWING ME.

IT'S NOT MY IMAGINATION.

COULD IT BE THE INARI FOX?

HE SOMETIMES SHOWS UP HERE, IN THE **HUMAN** WORLD.

THE INARI FOX OF THIS SHRINE IS QUITE MISCHIEVOUS.

OW!

125

PRESIDENT ARIA.

NYU.

FLOP

I'M A LITTLE SCARED.

JA-JING

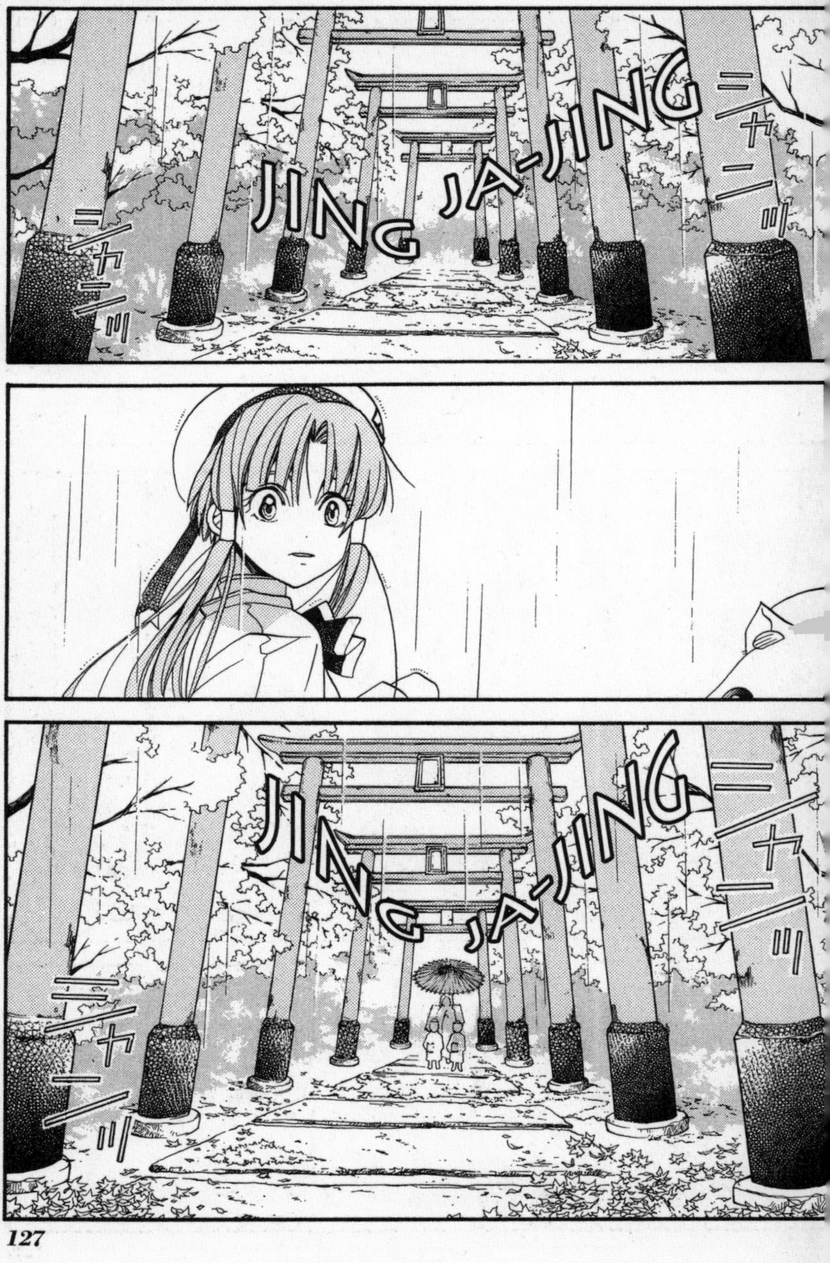
JING JA-JING
JING JA-JING

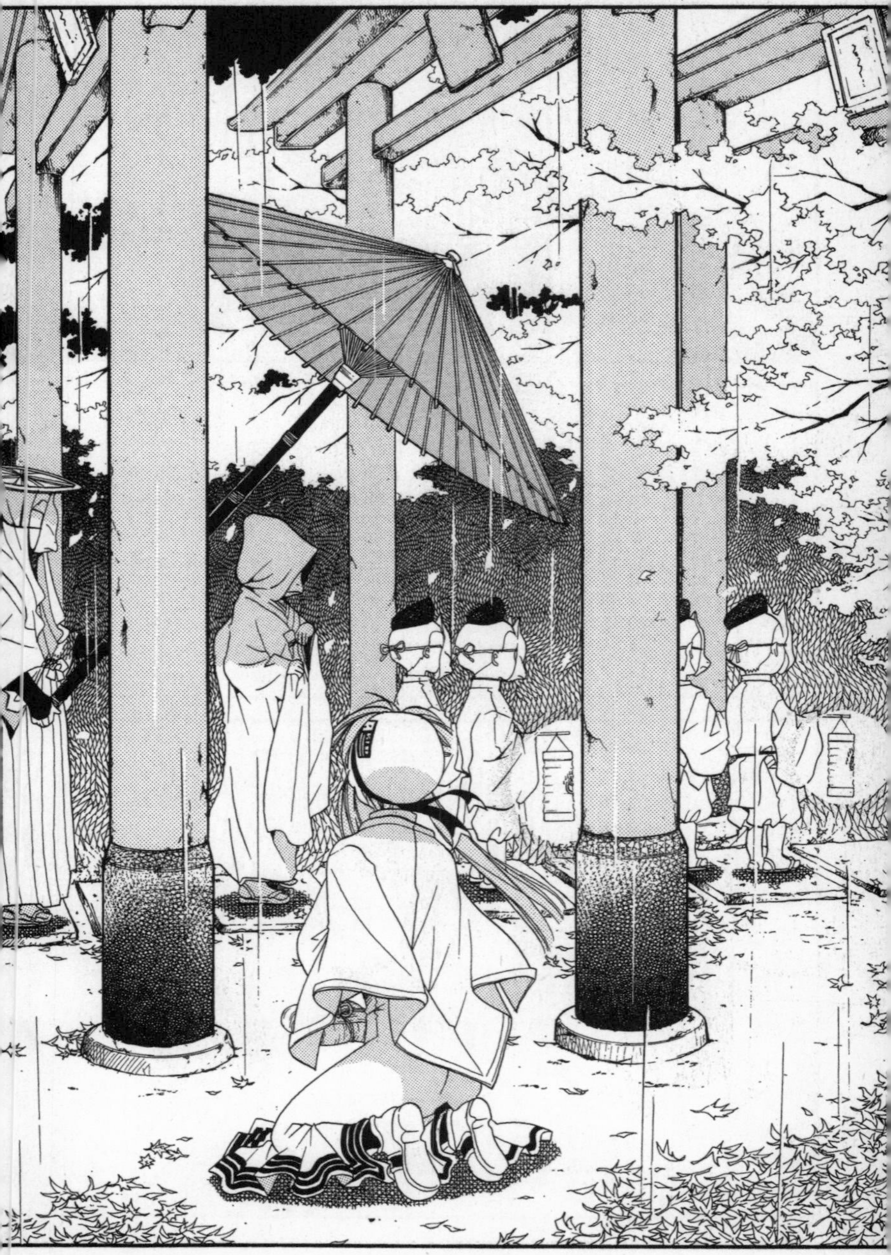

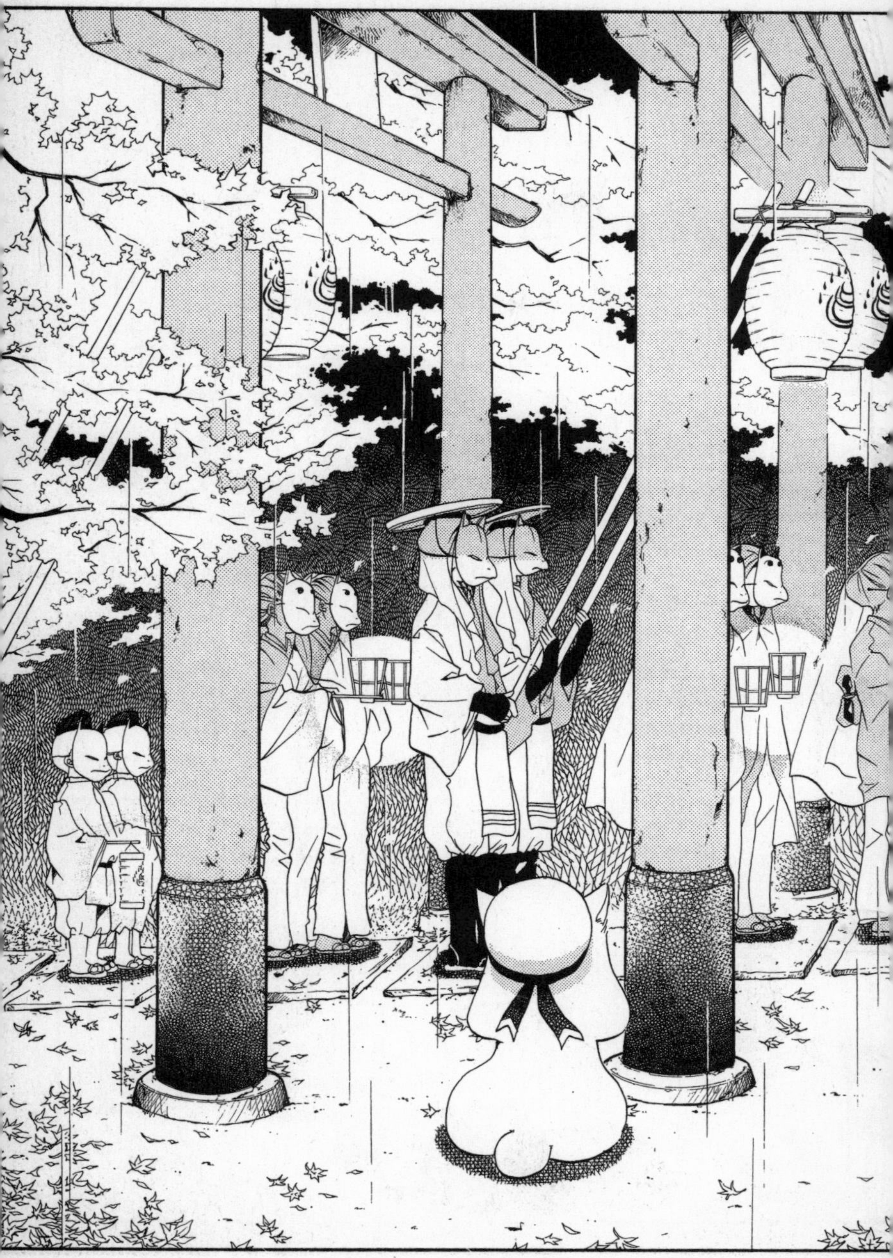

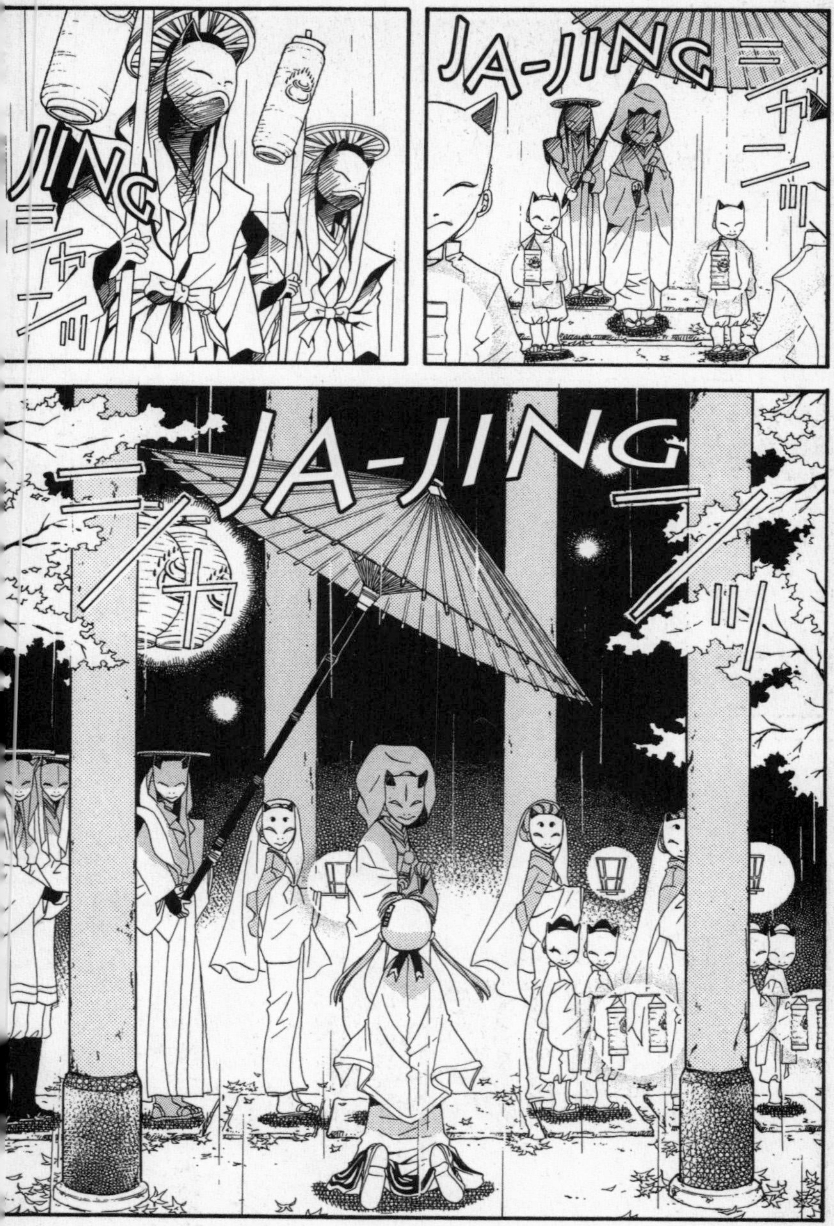
JA-JING
JING
JA-JING

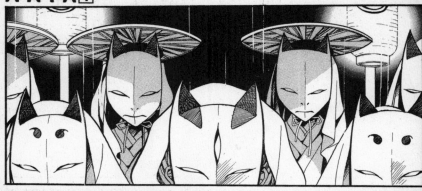

UH, WHA... UM

!

THWMP

AIII!

HUH?

WH, WHAT...

DO I DO NOW?

BA-DUMP

BA-DUMP

YOU CAN NEVER RETURN HERE AGAIN!

ONCE HE TAKES YOU...

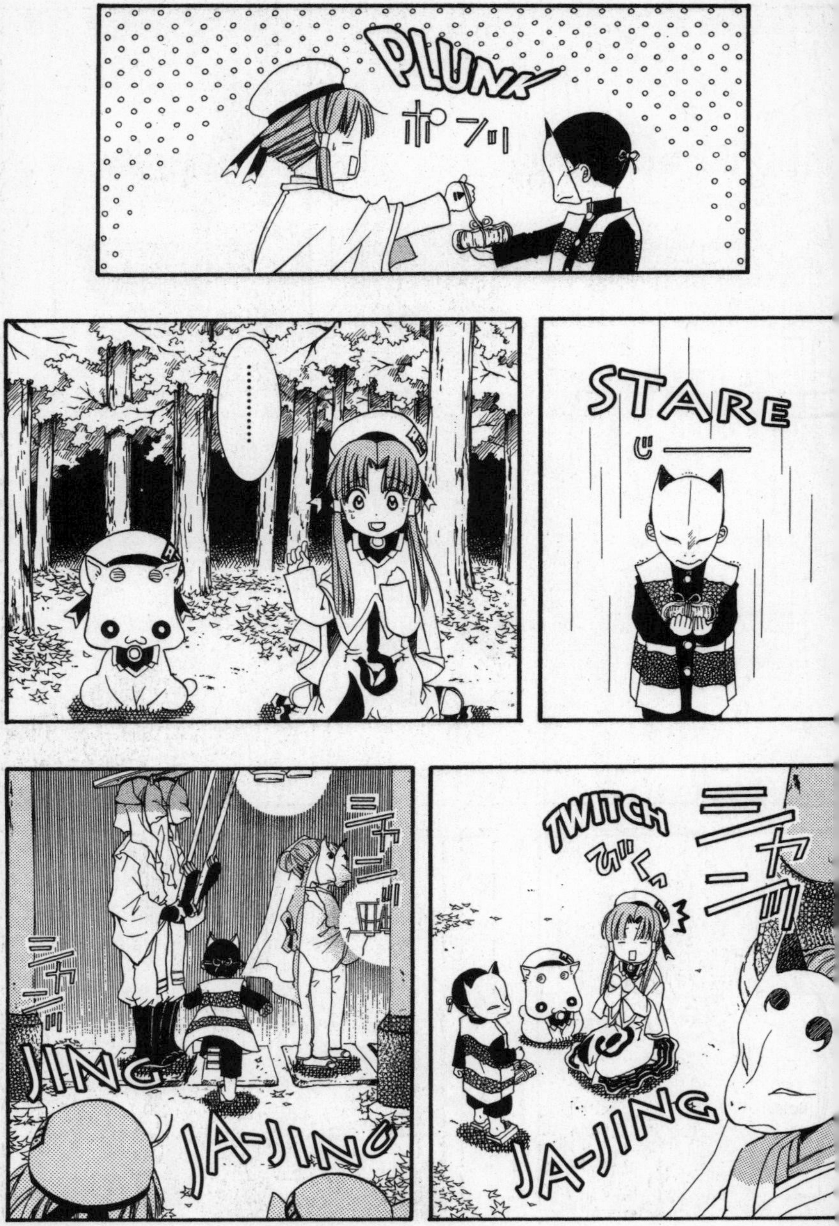
PLUNK
STARE
じーー
......
TWITCH
びくっ
JA-JING
JING
JA-JING

FWSSHH

JA-ING

JING

· · · · · · ·

SQUEEZE!

WHEN DID IT STOP?

HEY, IT STOPPED RAINING.

WELL, WELL. **YOU'VE** BEEN GONE AWHILE.

ERR, I SAW...

THE WEDDING PROCESSION OF THE INARI FOX!

FWUMP

MISS ALICIA!

I **THOUGHT** YOU'D COME BACK HERE IF YOU GOT LOST!

WELL, IT IS SUPPOSED TO BE THEIR FAVORITE FOOD.

THEY TOOK MY INARIZUSHI.

HA-HA-HA-HA

YES.

REALLY?

MAYBE IT'S BECAUSE OF MY FAMOUS INARIZUSHI.

IF YOU REALLY DID MEET AN INARI FOX...

OH, I ALMOST FORGOT.

GONG

MA'AM! CAN I HAVE 10 INARIZUSHI?

COMING RIGHT UP!

THEY'RE FOR ME!

HUH?

ISN'T THAT YOUR INARIZUSHI FROM EARLIER?

FWSSHHH

HOW DID IT GET HERE?

MAYBE ...

ALL HE WANTED...

I'M SORRY I WAS SO SCARED.

WAS TO HAVE SOME INARIZUSHI.

CLAP CLAP

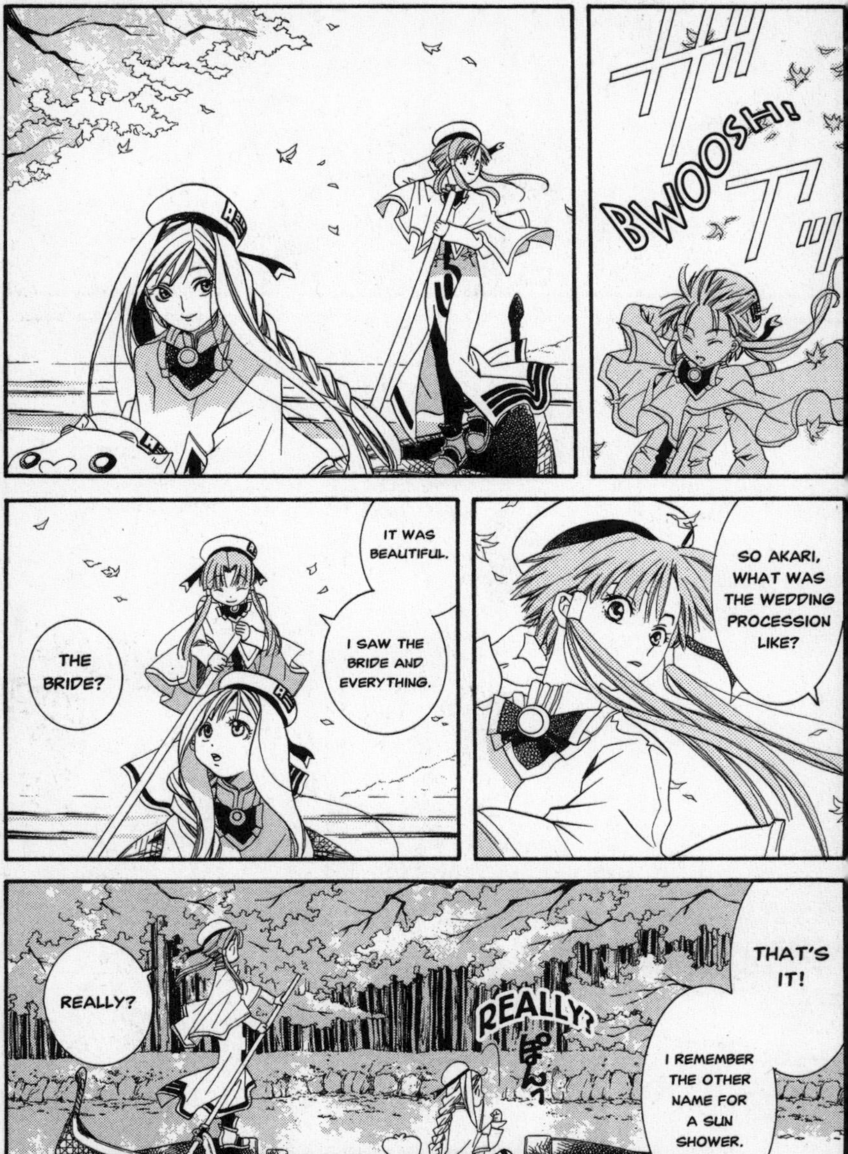
BWOOSH!
SO AKARI, WHAT WAS THE WEDDING PROCESSION LIKE?
IT WAS BEAUTIFUL.
I SAW THE BRIDE AND EVERYTHING.
THE BRIDE?
THAT'S IT!
I REMEMBER THE OTHER NAME FOR A SUN SHOWER.
REALLY?
REALLY?

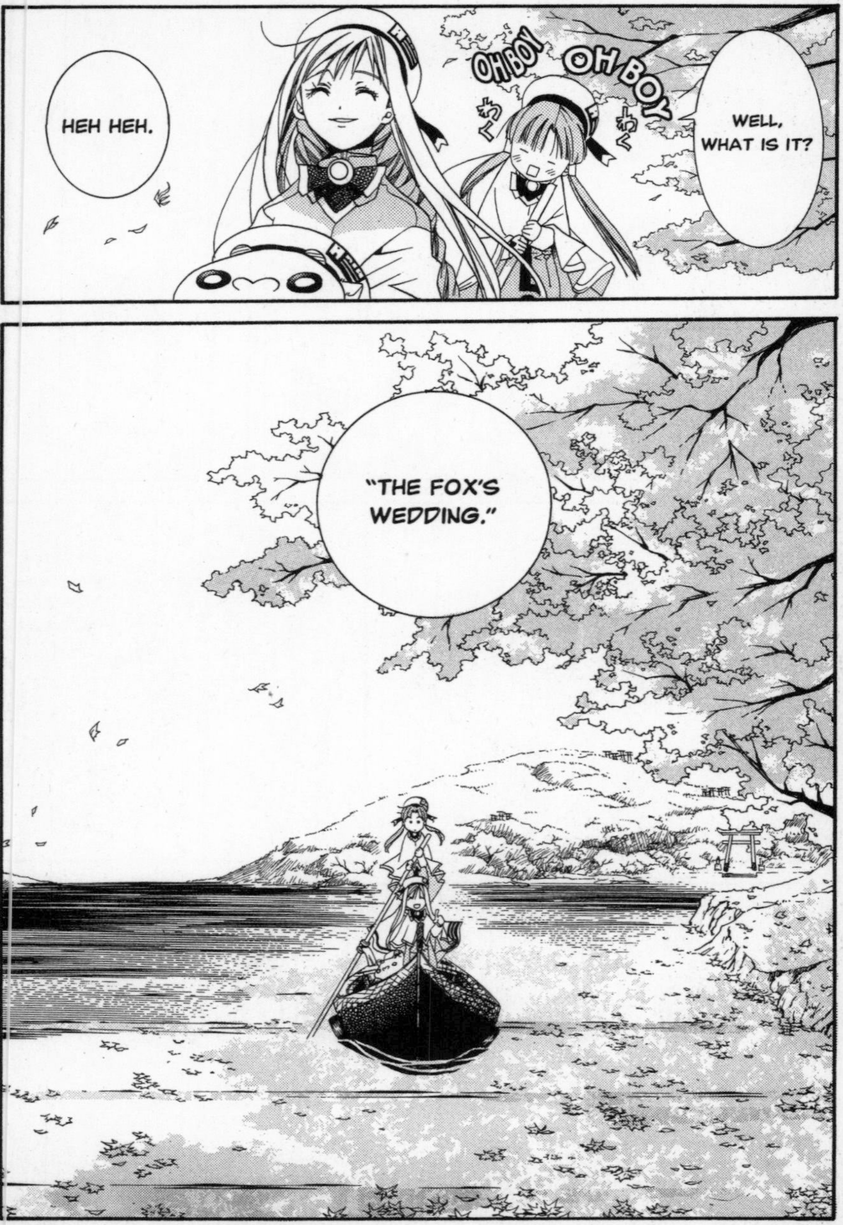
WELL, WHAT IS IT?
OH BOY OH BOY
わく わく
HEH HEH.
"THE FOX'S WEDDING."

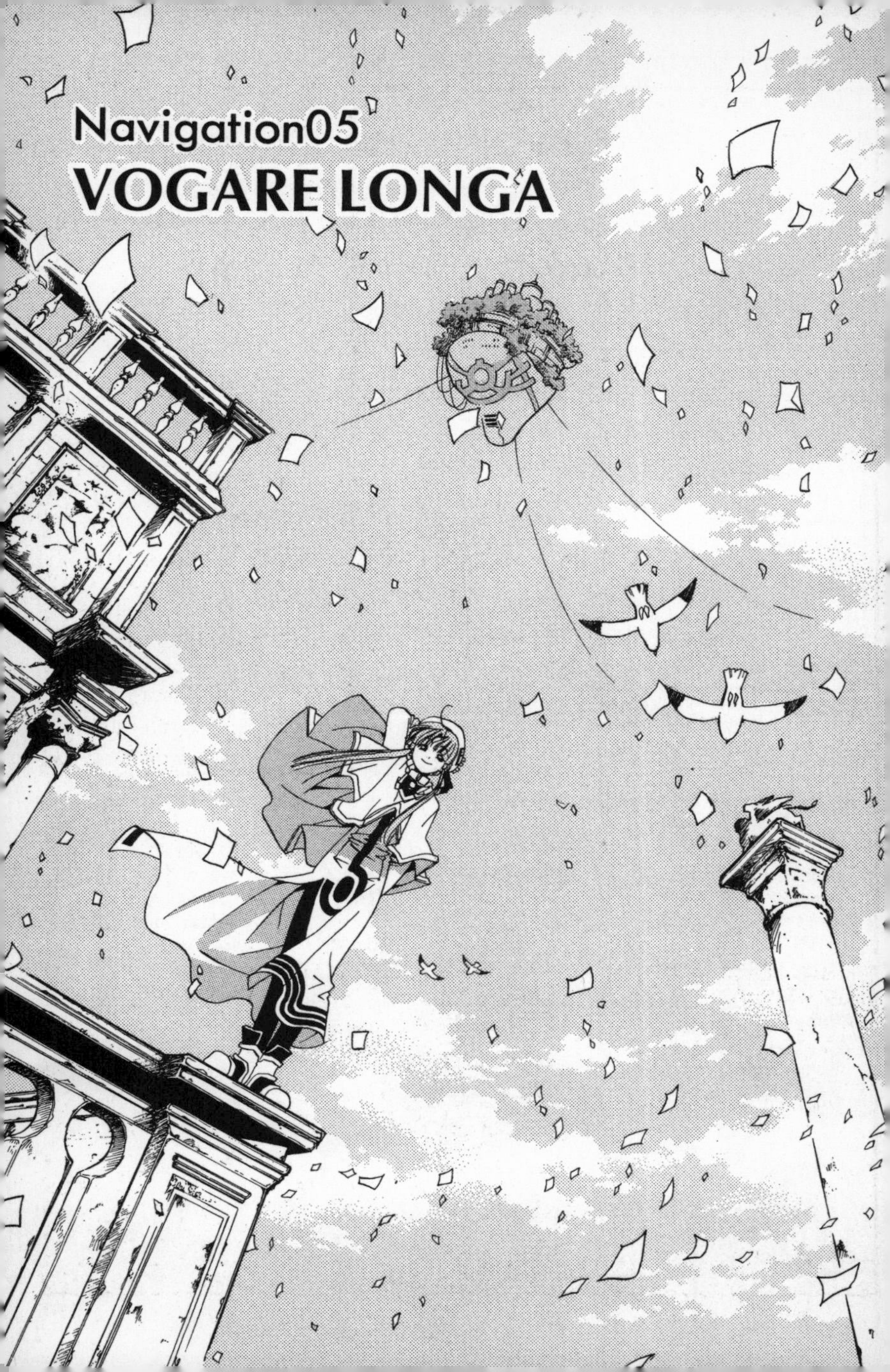
Navigation05
VOGARE LONGA

HELLO. HOW ARE YOU DOING?

THE LONG AUTUMN IS ABOUT TO END.

SQUEEZE

IT'S BEEN UNUSUALLY CROWDED AROUND HERE LATELY.

I WONDER WHY

THE WIND COMING ACROSS THE SEA HAS STARTED TO FEEL CHILLY.

OH, THERE YOU ARE.

練習 おつかれさま

HOW WAS PRACTICE?

I'M BACK, ALICIA!

YOU'RE PUTTING UP POSTERS?

HEH HEH.

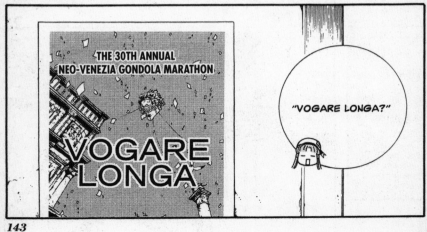

THE 30TH ANNUAL NEO-VENEZIA GONDOLA MARATHON

VOGARE LONGA

"VOGARE LONGA?"

143

I SEE...

IT'S A POSTER FOR THE **VOGARE LONGA**, A GONDOLA MARATHON. THE WHOLE TOWN'S GOING TO PARTICIPATE!

THAT'S RIGHT. *VOGARE* MEANS "TO ROW" AND *LONGA* MEANS "A LONG TIME."

THAT'S RIGHT! EVERYONE'S OUT PRACTICING FOR THE MARATHON.

NO WONDER THERE'VE BEEN SO MANY GONDOLAS ON THE RIVER LATELY.

THIS IS THE BIGGEST AUTUMN EVENT IN NEO-VENEZIA.

I'VE BEEN PUTTING THESE POSTERS UP EVERYWHERE.

BUT IT'S NOT ABOUT WHO WINS OR LOSES.

THIS FESTIVAL IS FOR **EVERYONE** WHO ENJOYS ROWING, PRO OR AMATEUR!

THE COURSE IS ABOUT 32 KILOMETERS LONG. IT'LL TAKE AT LEAST FOUR HOURS FOR THE FAST GONDOLAS TO FINISH.

THE SLOW ONES WILL TAKE ALMOST ALL DAY.

OF COURSE!

OH BOY! *&?♪♪

YOU MEAN, EVEN I COULD ENTER?

TAP TAP

WOW! I CAN'T WAIT!

?

SHREEE

SHREEE

OH. CRICKETS!

REEEE

REEE

REEEE

SHREE

THE VOGALONGA IS ALSO A SEASONAL EVENT. IT TELLS US THAT AUTUMN IS OFFICIALLY OVER.

ONCE THE RACE IS FINISHED...

SHREEE

REEEE

EVERYONE STARTS GETTING READY FOR WINTER.

...AND GOOD LUCK!

YOU'VE BEEN TRAINING A LOT RECENTLY. I HOPE WE GET TO **SEE** SOME OF THAT OUT THERE... TRY YOUR HARDEST, OKAY?

Welcome to ARIA COMPANY

I WILL!

REEEE

REEE

SHREE

IT'S NOT THAT EASY, AKARI!

SPLSSSH

IT'S A **TEST** TO SEE IF YOU HAVE WHAT IT TAKES TO BE A FULL-FLEDGED UNDINE.

BUT I'VE HEARD THAT FOR UNDINES IN TRAINING LIKE US,

WHAT?!

"EASY PEASY?"

HUH?

EASY PEASY'S NOT SO EASY!

TO **REGULAR** PEOPLE, THE VOGALONGA IS JUST A CONTEST.

WHEN WE MOVED UP FROM BEING NEW RECRUITS TO TRAINEES?

POINT!

IDIOT! DON'T YOU REMEMBER ...

BUT ALICIA DIDN'T SAY ANYTHING LIKE THAT.

SHE'S DONE IT BEFORE!

DID ALICIA MENTION ANYTHING ABOUT A "TEST" TO US THEN? **NO**!! IT WAS ALL A SURPRISE!

YOU'RE RIGHT.

THAT SETTLES IT.

TWINKLE

NOW THAT I THINK ABOUT IT, SHE **DID** SAY SOMETHING:

WELL, THEN...

"YOU'VE BEEN TRAINING A LOT RECENTLY. I HOPE WE GET TO SEE SOME OF THAT OUT THERE."

SORRY!

WORKING HARD ALL THIS TIME...

HEY, YOU'RE BLOCKING THE WAY!

LET'S DO IT!

TO BECOME FIRST-RATE UNDINES.

AND WITH ANY LUCK, IN 1ST PLACE!

IF THE VOGALONGA IS A TEST...

WE **MUST** FINISH IN THE TOP GROUP!

HUMPH!

AIKA AND I HAVE BEEN...

AKARI, THIS IS OUR CHANCE TO GET ONE STEP CLOSER TO BEING FULL-FLEDGED UNDINES!

IT MIGHT BE JUST A RUMOR, BUT WE CAN'T TAKE ANY CHANCES. WE HAVE TO GIVE IT OUR ALL.

ALRIGHT!

SPLSSHH

GLOVES HAVE A LOT TO DO WITH YOUR SKILL LEVEL AS AN UNDINE.

"ONE STEP CLOSER," HUH?

REEE

SHREEE

THE LESS BLISTERS YOU GET ON YOUR PALMS.

THE BETTER YOU GET AT ROWING A GONDOLA,

DURING YOUR INITIAL TRAINING, YOU WEAR GLOVES ON BOTH HANDS.

THEN YOU BECOME A TRAINEE AND USE JUST ONE GLOVE.

YOU BECOME A FULL-FLEDGED UNDINE.

FINALLY, YOU DON'T NEED **ANY** GLOVES AT ALL.

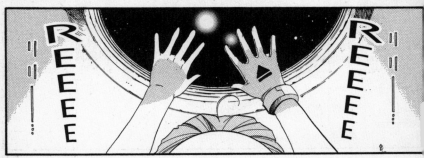

REEEE

REEEE

BY THE WAY, AIKA AND I WEAR **ONE** GLOVE, SO THAT MEANS WE'RE TRAINEES.

CLICK

CLICK

HM!

NYU!

I'M GONNA TRY MY HARDEST!

NYU?

PRESIDENT ARIA.

AN EXCELLENT UNDINE!

SHREEE

REEE

THEY'LL SEE. ONE DAY, I'M GOING TO BE...

CLICK

HELLO EVERYONE, AND WELCOME TO THE 30TH ANNUAL VOGALONGA.

THIS IS IT, THE MAJOR EVENT THAT MARKS THE END OF AUTUMN IN NEO-VENEZIA.

WE WILL SOON BE GETTING UNDERWAY.

WOW!

POP!

BA-BANG!

153

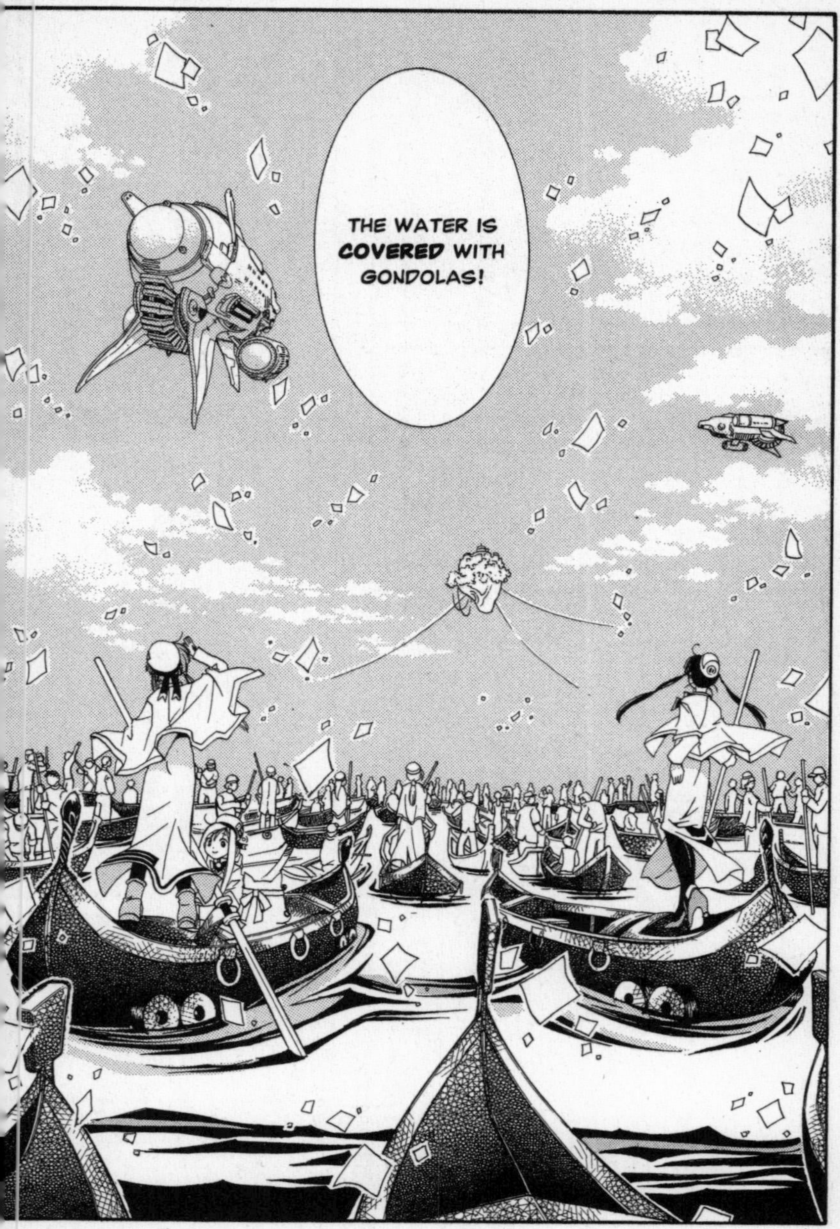
THE WATER IS COVERED WITH GONDOLAS!

OH BOY OH BO~

BA-DUM!

ドキ
ドキ

BA-DUM!

· · · · · · · ·

WHY'D YOU BRING PRESIDENT ARIA?

HE SAID HE WANTS TO BE IN IT, TOO.

CONCENTRATE ON THE RACE!

BEHAVING HERSELF IN FRONT OF ALICIA.

YANK

THIS IS NO TIME TO BE GOOFING OFF!

TOSS!

THERE!

HEY, MY FLAG!

FLAP FLAP

ぱた ぱた
わ～た

WAAUGH

HE'S JUST GOING TO WEIGH YOU DOWN.

? HAVE YOU FORGOTTEN HOW IMPORTANT THIS RACE IS TO OUR CAREERS?

SORRY.

AKARI! AIKA!

YES?

GET IT TOGETHER, WILL YOU?

NO, NO!

I JUST GOT SO WRAPPED UP IN ALL THOSE GONDOLAS, AND...

I DON'T THINK SHE HAS A CLUE...

JITTER

JITTER

HAVE FUN, AND DO YOUR BEST!

I WON'T LET YOU DOWN.

AT LEAST, NOT ABOUT THE ENJOYING PART.

WE WILL!

BA-DUMP

BA-DUMP

BAAAAANG!

FIDGET

YAAAAAAAAY!

THE RACE IS ABOUT TO BEGIN!

TAKE YOUR POSITIONS. READY —

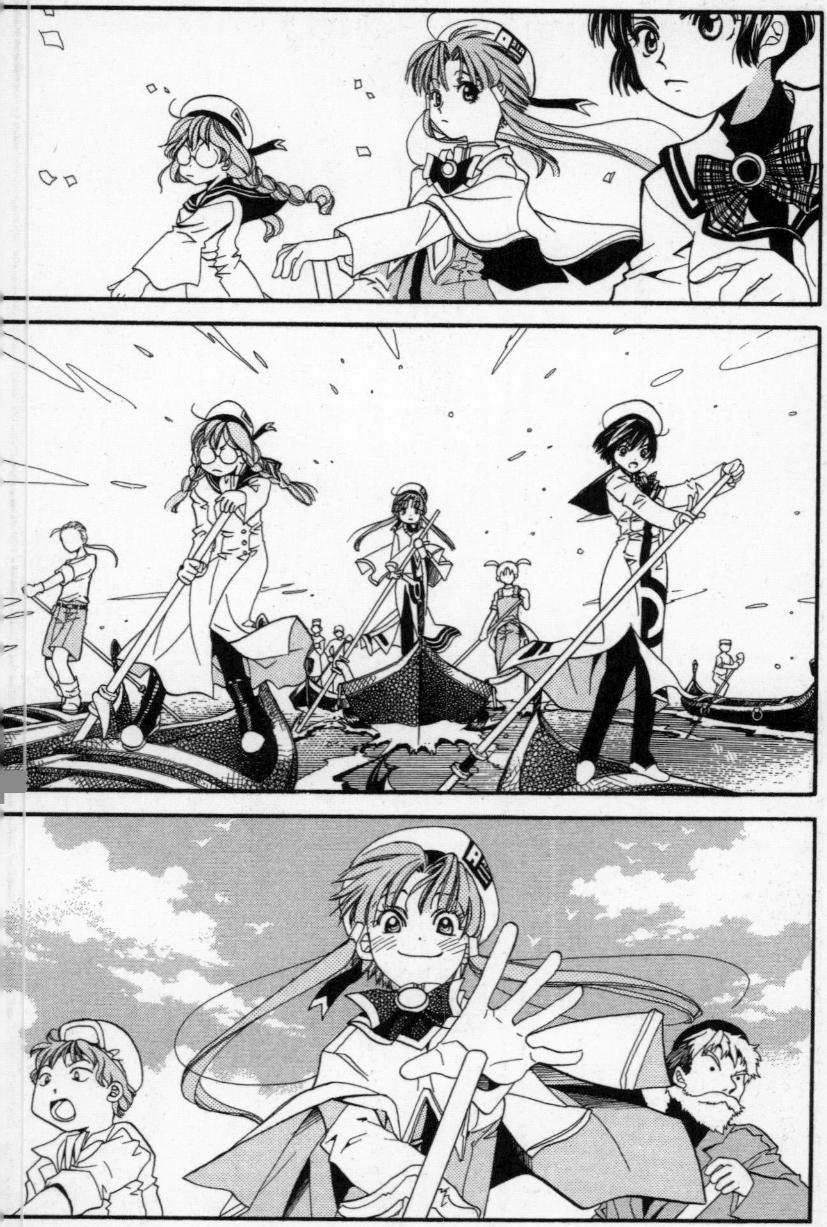

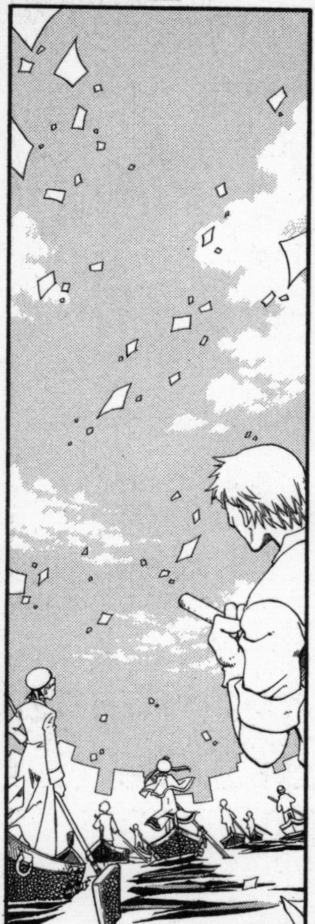

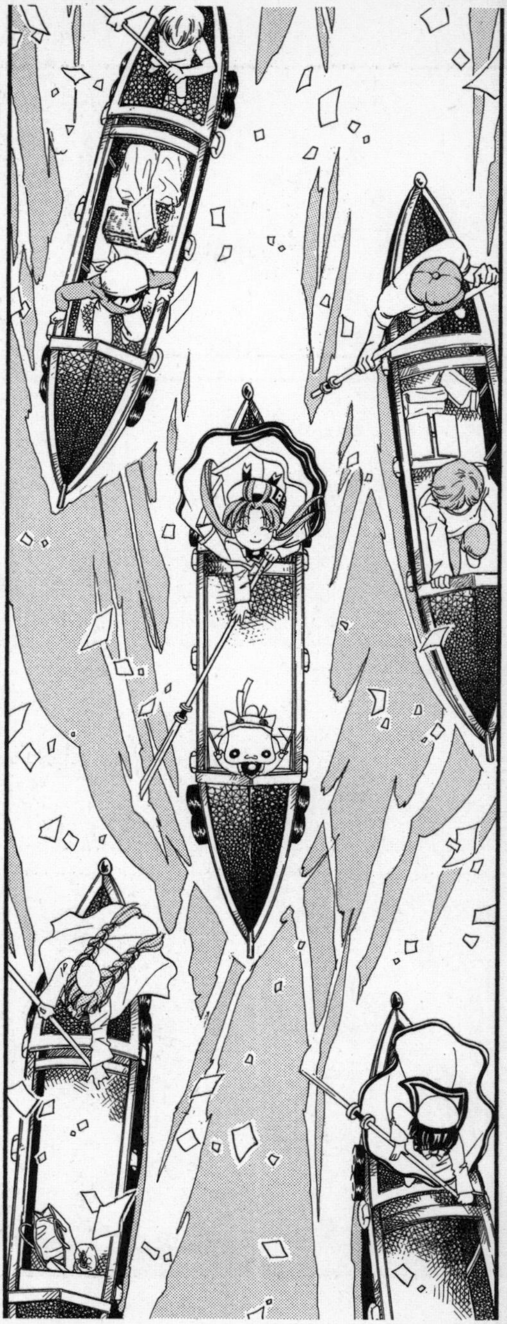

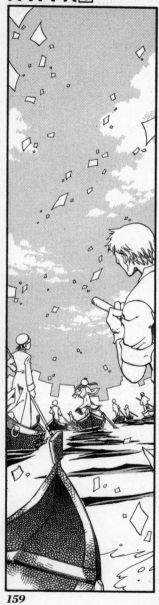

HEY!

ＨＹＡＡＡＡＹ！

HI THERE!

郵便屋の おじさんだー

THE POSTMAN!

HEY, MISS!

THANK YOU!

GOOD LUCK!

WAVE WAVE WAVE WAVE

GRARR!

WAVE WAVE WAVE

SORRY!

HEH HEH HEH. I JUST CAN'T HELP IT. I'M HAVING SO MUCH FUN!

JEEZ...

CONCENTRATE ON THE RACE!

LET'S GO!

ROGER!

ALRIGHT, NOW PUT YOUR GAME FACE ON.

PRESIDENT ARIA, LOOK AT ALL THESE GONDOLAS!

NYU.

THANKS!

BOOM!

BA-BOOM!

YAAAAAH!

SPLOOSH!!

DIDN'T EVEN NOTICE...

おりゃりゃ
GO! GO, GO!!!

UH-OH.

GLUB GLUB
ぶくぶく

DON'T WORRY ABOUT IT!

UMM...

UM...

AAAAH!

I TOLD YOU IT'S OKAY!

GLUB
どんぶら
どんぶら
GLUB

HEY, YOU'RE IN THE MIDDLE OF A RACE! HURRY UP!

A IT'S JUST A RUMOR, BUT...

I'VE HEARD THAT THE VOGALONGA IS LIKE A PROMOTION TEST FOR UNDINES.

HMM HMM HMM

ふん ふん ふん ♪

I'M SO SORRY...

BUT ARE YOU **SURE** YOU SHOULD BE DOING THIS?

WHAT?!

YEAH.

I HEARD THE SAME RUMOR BEFORE, TOO.

WHY?

DON'T WORRY, I'LL BE DONE IN A SEC.

WHAT IF THE RUMOR IS TRUE?

本当だったらどうするの〜い

WELL, WHAT ARE YOU STILL DOING HERE?! HURRY UP!

WELL THEN...

WAIT A MINUTE!

BESIDES, I DON'T WANT THIS FRUIT TO GO TO WASTE. ♡

THAT'S ALL OF THEM.

•••••••

はい 終わりっと

164

ARIA ①

I'LL BE USING YOUR SERVICE FROM NOW ON!

YOU'RE FROM ARIA COMPANY, RIGHT?

YES, MA'AM.

BOOM

BA-BOOM

YOU'RE WELCOME!

THANK YOU VERY MUCH!

拾ってくれて
ありがとー

THANKS FOR YOUR HELP!

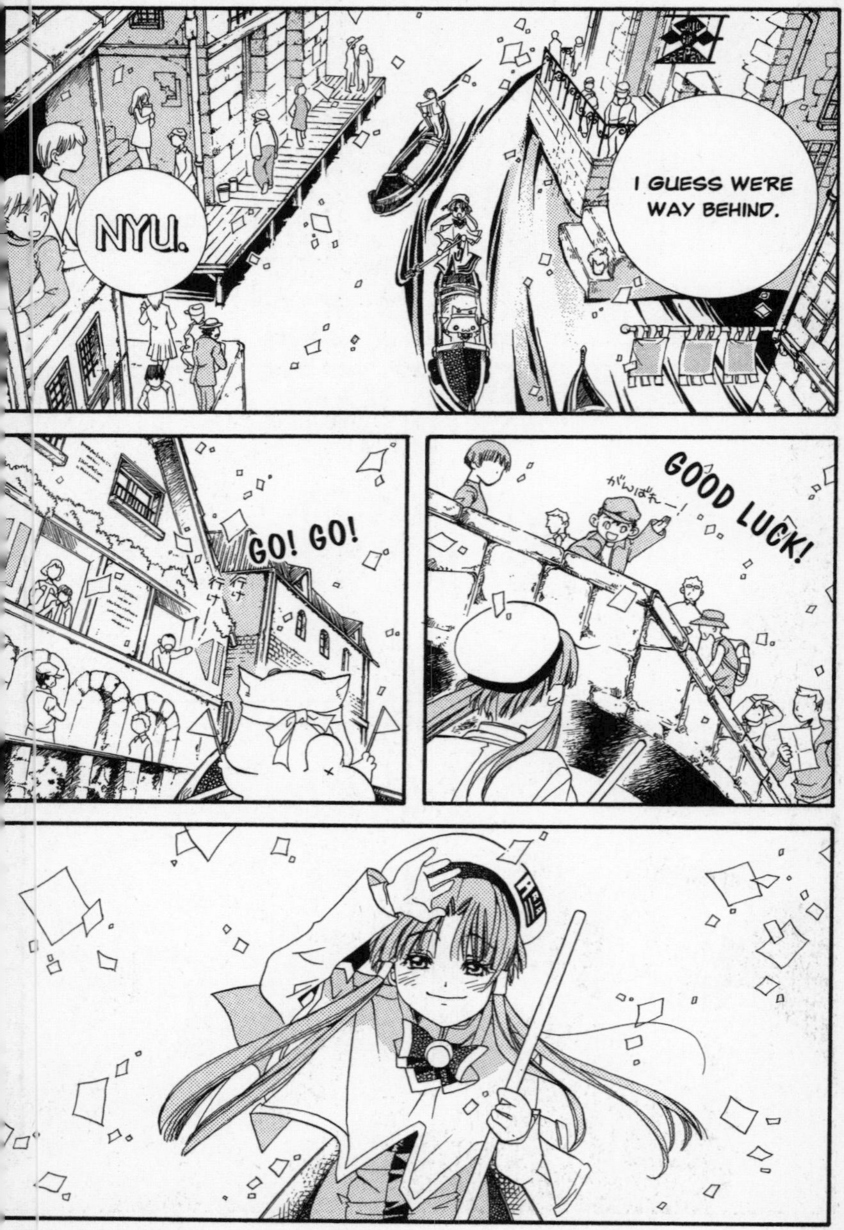

I GUESS WE'RE WAY BEHIND.
NYU.
GOOD LUCK!
がんばれー!
GO! GO!
行け行けー!

PRESIDENT ARIA?

NYU?

I COULD JUST KEEP ON...

I WISH...

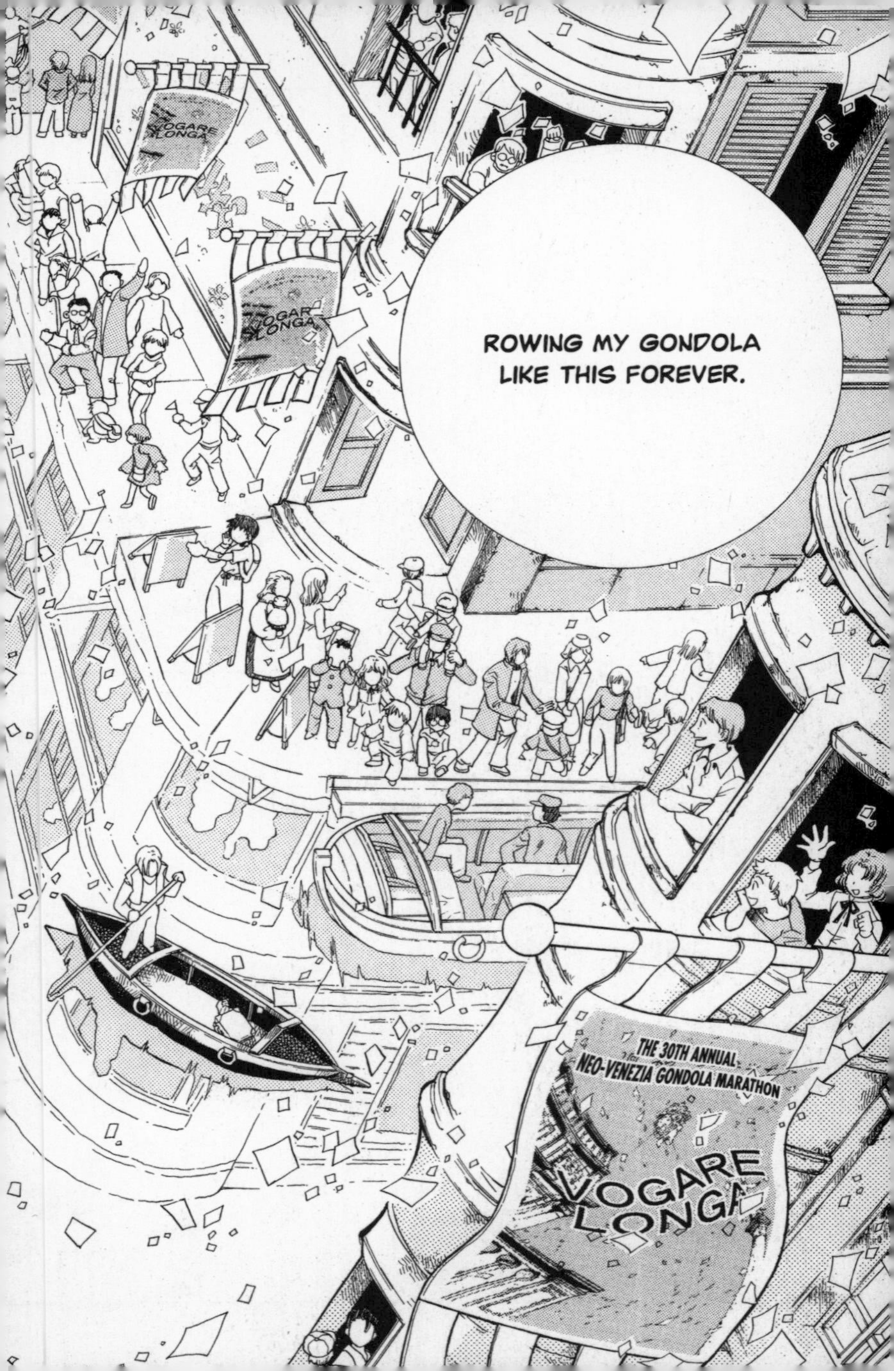
ROWING MY GONDOLA LIKE THIS FOREVER.
THE 30TH ANNUAL NEO-VENEZIA GONDOLA MARATHON
VOGARE

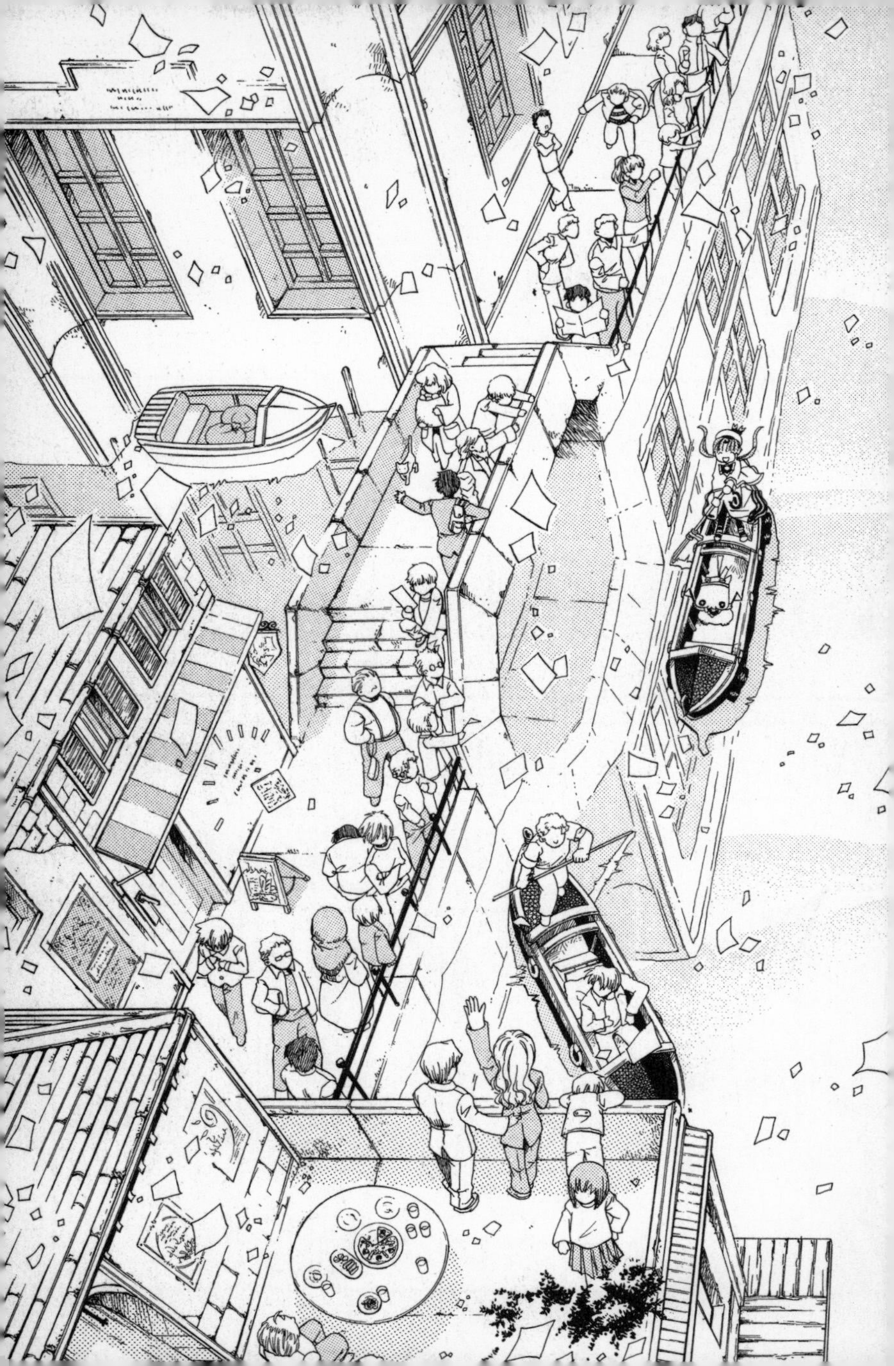

BOOM

BA-BOOM

GOAL!

HEY THERE!

AIKA!

AKARI! ARE YOU OUT OF YOUR MIND?!

THIS COULD'VE BEEN YOUR CHANCE TO ADVANCE AS AN UNDINE!

HOW ARE YOU GONNA EXPLAIN THIS TO ALICIA?

I LOOKED BACK AND YOU WERE, LIKE, GONE!

I CAN'T BELIEVE YOU TOOK ALL DAY TO FINISH THE RACE!

smack

WHAT WERE YOU THINKING?!

OUCH!

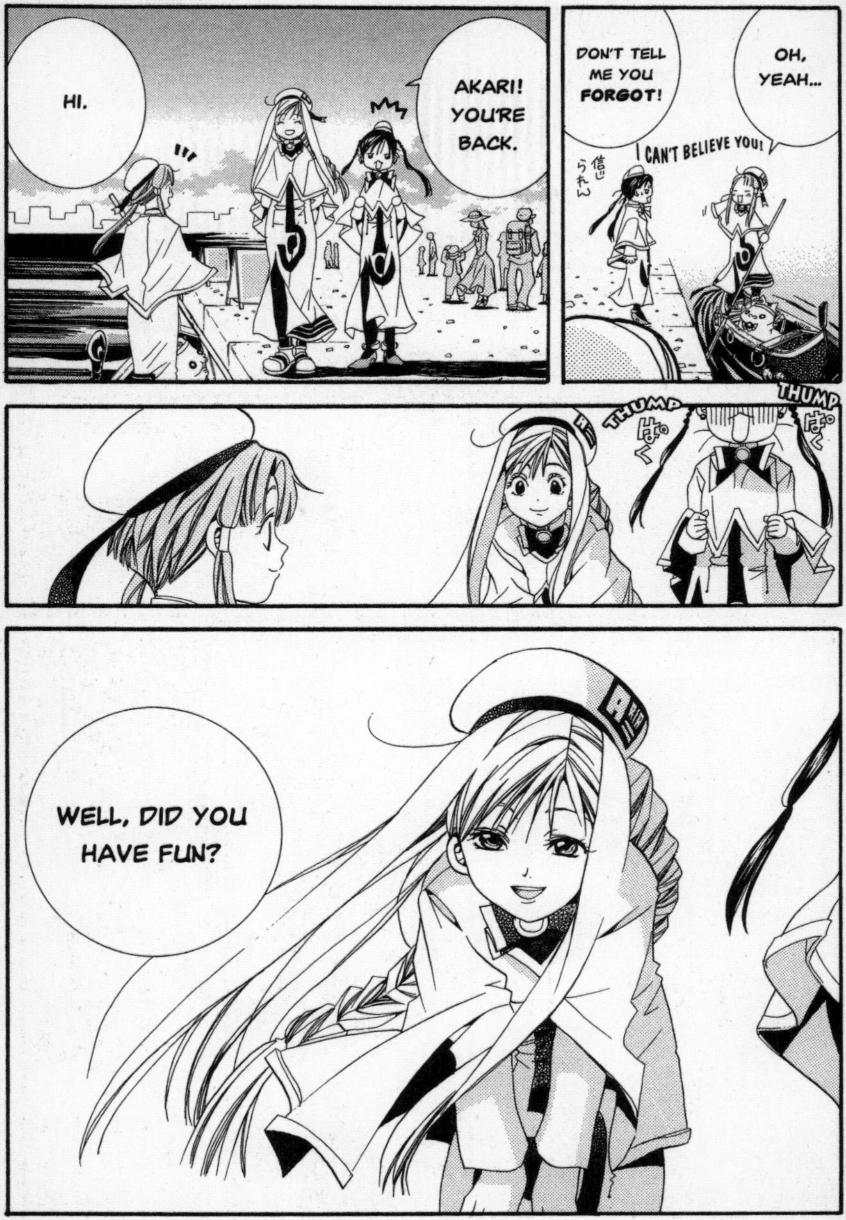
AKARI! YOU'RE BACK.
HI.
OH, YEAH...
DON'T TELL ME YOU FORGOT!
I CAN'T BELIEVE YOU!
信じられん
THUMP
ぱく
THUMP
ぱく
WELL, DID YOU HAVE FUN?

THUS ENDED MY FIRST VOGALONGA.

TO TELL YOU THE TRUTH,

BUT I WAS HAVING SO MUCH FUN...

I NEVER FORGOT IT WAS A TEST.

IT MIGHT TAKE A LITTLE LONGER...

I DIDN'T WANT IT TO END.

BUT I WANT TO BECOME A FULL-FLEDGED UNDINE AT MY **OWN** PACE.

AND I SHOULD HAVE FUN WHILE I'M AT IT, RIGHT?

SHOCK!!

NAAH, THAT'S JUST A RUMOR.

IT'S A LIE

ALICIA, WE HEARD THAT THE VOGALONGA IS REALLY A TEST FOR WOULD-BE UNDINES.

ARIA 1 END

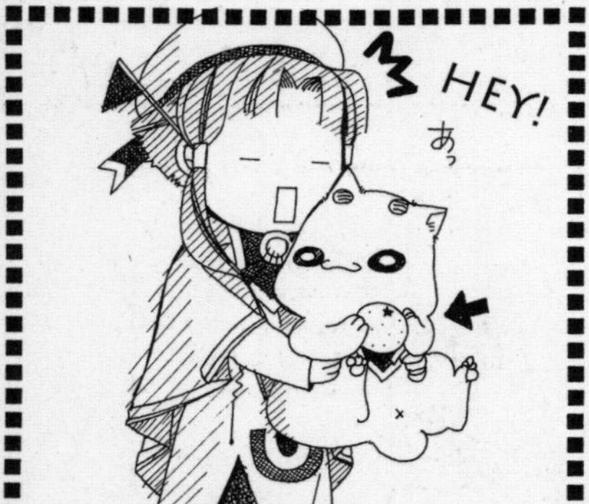
HEY!
あっ

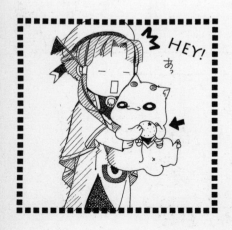

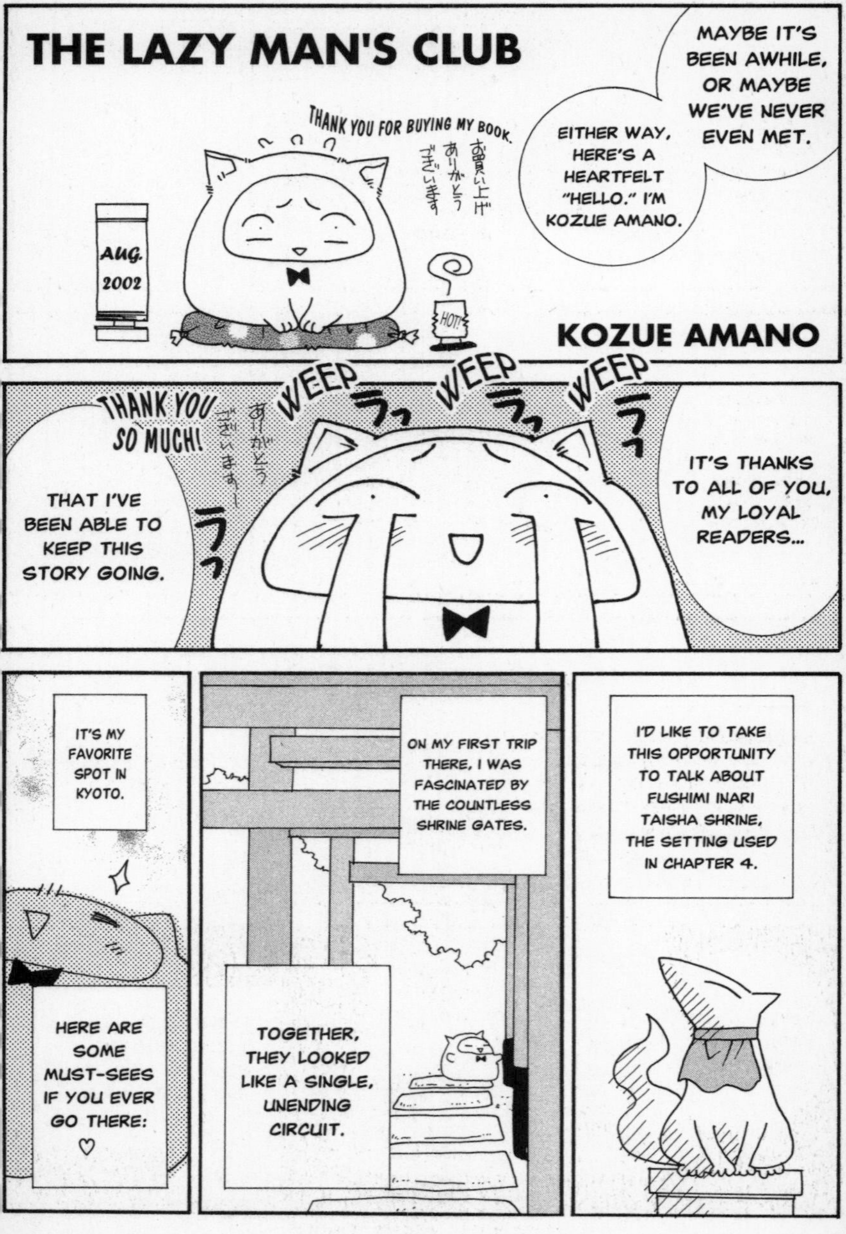
THE LAZY MAN'S CLUB
KOZUE AMANO
MAYBE IT'S BEEN AWHILE, OR MAYBE WE'VE NEVER EVEN MET.
EITHER WAY, HERE'S A HEARTFELT "HELLO." I'M KOZUE AMANO.
THANK YOU FOR BUYING MY BOOK.
お買い上げありがとうございます
AUG. 2002
HOT!
IT'S THANKS TO ALL OF YOU, MY LOYAL READERS...
WEEP WEEP WEEP
THAT I'VE BEEN ABLE TO KEEP THIS STORY GOING.
THANK YOU SO MUCH!
ありがとうございます～
I'D LIKE TO TAKE THIS OPPORTUNITY TO TALK ABOUT FUSHIMI INARI TAISHA SHRINE, THE SETTING USED IN CHAPTER 4.
ON MY FIRST TRIP THERE, I WAS FASCINATED BY THE COUNTLESS SHRINE GATES.
TOGETHER, THEY LOOKED LIKE A SINGLE, UNENDING CIRCUIT.
IT'S MY FAVORITE SPOT IN KYOTO.
HERE ARE SOME MUST-SEES IF YOU EVER GO THERE: ♡

CHK CHK

IF YOU BUY ONE, THEY'LL LIGHT IT FOR YOU.

CAN YOU BELIEVE THEY MAKE THEM BY HAND?

THEY'RE REALLY QUITE IMPRESSIVE.

THEY'VE GOT A REALLY BIG WICK, SO OF COURSE THE FLAME GETS BIG, TOO.

WA-CANDLE

#1

THE CLOSER THE WEIGHT IS TO WHAT YOU THOUGHT, THE MORE LIKELY YOUR WISH IS TO COME TRUE.

OMOKARU STONE

AFTER MAKING A WISH, YOU LIFT THE STONE, THINKING TO YOURSELF EITHER "BE HEAVY" OR "BE LIGHT."

OMOKARU STONE

#2

SOME ARE EXCITING, AND SOME ARE HEARTWARMING. I HOPE SOME OF THAT SAME KIND OF FEELING COMES THROUGH IN MY WORK.

THERE ARE SO MANY WONDERFUL PLACES LIKE THIS IN THE WORLD.

THANK YOU FOR YOUR SUPPORT!

I HOPE TO SEE YOU AGAIN IN VOLUME 2!

WITHOUT YOU, DEAR READERS, I WOULDN'T BE MAKING THIS MANGA AT ALL. THANK YOU!

SEE YOU NEXT TIME!

ARIA VOLUME ONE

©KOZUE AMANO 2002
All Rights Reserved
First published in 2002 by Mag Garden Co., Ltd., Tokyo, Japan.
English translation rights arranged with Mag Garden Co., Ltd.

Translator	**KAY BERTRAND**
Lead Translator/Translation Supervisor	**JAVIER LOPEZ**
ADV Manga Translation Staff	**AMY FORSYTH, BRENDAN FRAYNE and EIKO McGREGOR**
Print Production/ Art Studio Manager	**LISA PUCKETT**
Art Production Manager	**RYAN MASON**
Sr. Designer/Creative Manager	**JORGE ALVARADO**
Graphic Designer/Group Leader	**SHANNON RASBERRY**
Graphic Designer	**NANAKO TSUKIHASHI**
Graphic Artists	**CHRIS LAPP, KRISTINA MILESKI, NATALIA MORALES and LANCE SWARTOUT**
International Coordinator	**TORU IWAKAMI**
International Coordinator	**ATSUSHI KANBAYASHI**
Publishing Editor	**SUSAN ITIN**
Assistant Editor	**MARGARET SCHAROLD**
Editorial Assistant	**VARSHA BHUCHAR**
Proofreader	**SHERIDAN JACOBS**
Research/ Traffic Coordinator	**MARSHA ARNOLD**
President, C.E.O & Publisher	**JOHN LEDFORD**

Email: editor@adv-manga.com
www.adv-manga.com
www.advfilms.com

For sales and distribution inquiries please call 1.800.282.7202

ADV MANGA is a division of A.D. Vision, Inc.
10114 W. Sam Houston Parkway, Suite 200, Houston, Texas 77099
English text © 2004 published by A.D. Vision, Inc. under exclusive license.
ADV MANGA is a trademark of A.D. Vision, Inc.

ISBN: 1-4139-0040-2
First printing, April 2004
10 9 8 7 6 5 4 3 2 1
Printed in Canada

LETTER FROM THE ADV MANGA TRANSLATION STAFF

Dear Reader,

On behalf of the ADV Manga translation team, thank you for purchasing an ADV book. We are enthusiastic and committed to our work, and strive to carry our enthusiasm over into the book you hold in your hands.

Our goal is to retain the true spirit of the original Japanese book. While great care has been taken to render a true and accurate translation, some cultural or readability issues may require a line to be adapted for greater accessibility to our readers. At times, manga titles that include culturally-specific concepts will feature a "Translator's Notes" section, which explains noteworthy references to the original text.

We hope our commitment to a faithful translation is evident in every ADV book you purchase.

Sincerely,

Javier Lopez
Lead Translator

Eiko McGregor

Kay Bertrand

Brendan Frayne

Amy Forsyth

Aria Vol 01

Pg. 15

Man Home

Throughout this manga, the Japanese word for "Earth" is assigned the phonetic reading of "Man Home." In contrast to this is the newscast on page three, which plainly states "Earth" in English. This gives the impression that Man Home is a nickname for Earth, or perhaps an appellation used by the citizens of Aqua. In a nod to the latter theory, we had Akari initially use "Man Home," but then correct herself when she remembers she's talking to an offworlder.

Pg. 22

Baked Potatoes

In Japanese, this dish is *jagaimo butter*, or baked potatoes topped with butter.

Pg. 94

The Bridge of Sighs

The story that Akari tells was popularized by the Romantic poet Lord Byron, who conceived the name "Bridge of Sighs" some 300 years after the structure had been built.

Pg. 80

Winged lion

The winged lion originally appeared in Ezekiel 1:10, but later came to be the symbol of St. Mark. The association is said to have begun in a passage (Mark 1:3) where St. Mark describes John the Baptist as having a "voice crying out in the wilderness."

Pg. 108

Inari Fox

Some believe that the fox is an envoy of the harvest god, Inari.

Pg. 109

Inarizushi

Inarizushi is fried bean curd stuffed with sushi rice. It is supposed to be the favorite food of foxes, the envoys of Inari (hence the name).

Pg. 110

The Inari Fox of this shrine is quite mischievous

The fox is a common character in Japanese folklore, and is considered the most cunning of creatures. It is even said to be able to transform itself into different forms, including a human.

Pg. 138

Clapping

It is traditional to clap twice when offering a prayer at a shrine.

Pg. 140

The Fox's Wedding

Japanese legend says that on days when there is a sun shower, you may see the wedding procession of a young fox couple. Some areas of Japan hold festivals which re-create the fox wedding to give thanks for a rich harvest and pray for success in business.

Pg. 142

Vogalonga / Vogare Longa

The Vogalonga is an actual rowing competition held in Venice. *Vogare* is the infinitive form of the verb meaning "to row."

ARIA

2

The Further Adventures of a Neo-Venezian Gondolier

Coming July 2004

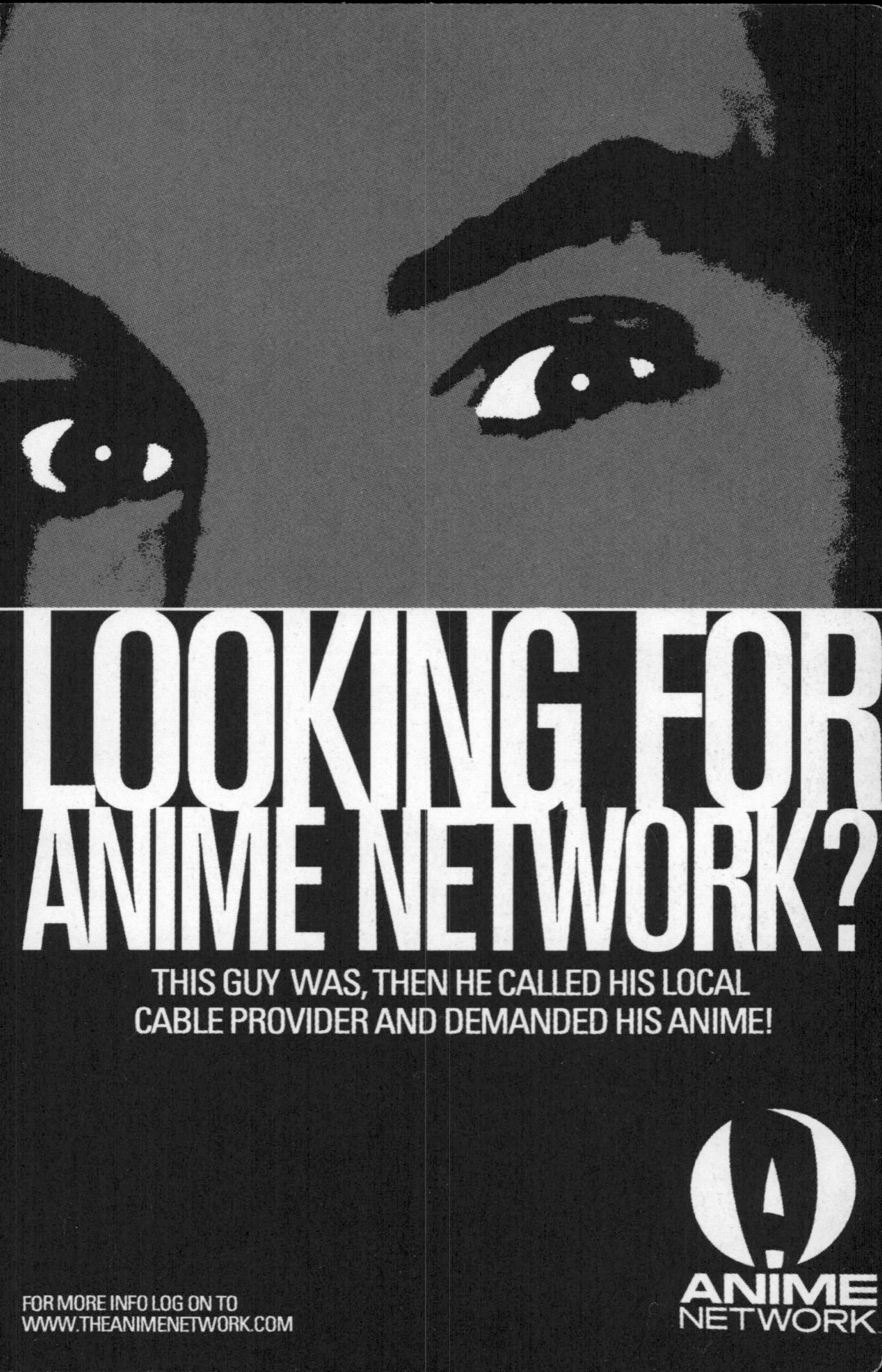
LOOKING FOR ANIME NETWORK?
THIS GUY WAS, THEN HE CALLED HIS LOCAL CABLE PROVIDER AND DEMANDED HIS ANIME!
ANIME NETWORK
FOR MORE INFO LOG ON TO
WWW.THEANIMENETWORK.COM

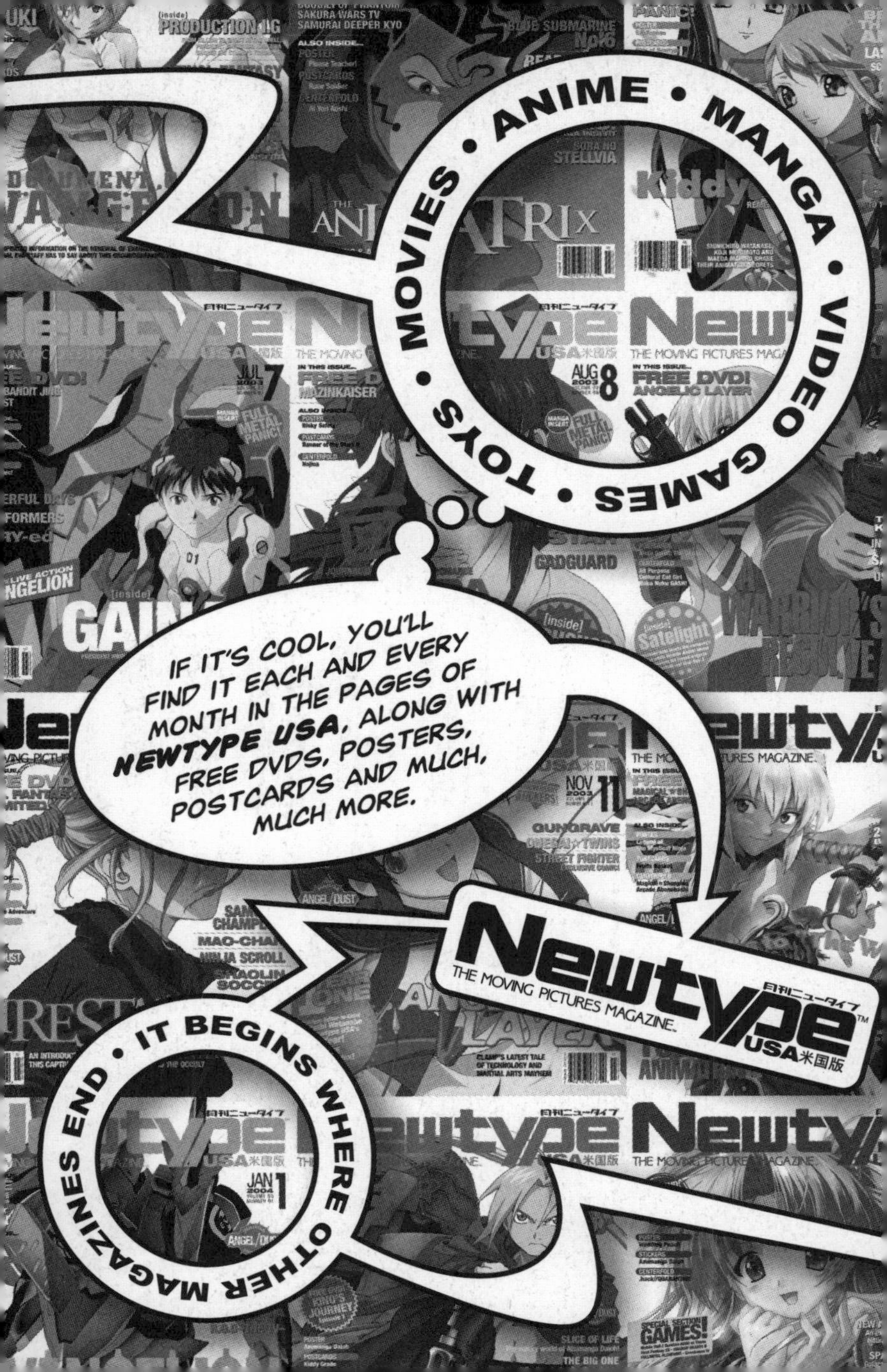
MOVIES • ANIME • MANGA • VIDEO GAMES • TOYS •
IF IT'S COOL, YOU'LL FIND IT EACH AND EVERY MONTH IN THE PAGES OF NEWTYPE USA, ALONG WITH FREE DVDS, POSTERS, POSTCARDS AND MUCH, MUCH MORE.
Newtype USA 米国版 THE MOVING PICTURES MAGAZINE. 月刊ニュータイプ
IT BEGINS WHERE OTHER MAGAZINES END •

MANGA SURVEY

PLEASE MAIL THE COMPLETED FORM TO: EDITOR – ADV MANGA
℅ A.D. Vision, Inc. 10114 W. Sam Houston Pkwy., Suite 200 Houston, TX 77099

Name:_____

Address:_____

City, State, Zip:_____

E-Mail:_____

Male ☐   Female ☐   Age:_____

☐ *CHECK HERE IF YOU WOULD LIKE TO RECEIVE OTHER INFORMATION OR FUTURE OFFERS FROM ADV.*

All information provided will be used for internal purposes only. We promise not to sell or otherwise divulge your information.

1. Annual Household Income (*Check only one*)
- ☐ Under $25,000
- ☐ $25,000 to $50,000
- ☐ $50,000 to $75,000
- ☐ Over $75,000

2. How do you hear about new Manga releases? (*Check all that apply*)
- ☐ Browsing in Store
- ☐ Internet Reviews
- ☐ Anime News Websites
- ☐ Direct Email Campaigns
- ☐ Magazine Ad
- ☐ Online Advertising
- ☐ Conventions
- ☐ TV Advertising
- ☐ Online forums (message boards and chat rooms)
- ☐ Carrier pigeon
- ☐ Other:_____

3. Which magazines do you read? (*Check all that apply*)
- ☐ Wizard
- ☐ SPIN
- ☐ Animerica
- ☐ Rolling Stone
- ☐ Maxim
- ☐ DC Comics
- ☐ URB
- ☐ Polygon
- ☐ Original Play Station Magazine
- ☐ Entertainment Weekly
- ☐ YRB
- ☐ EGM
- ☐ Newtype USA
- ☐ SciFi
- ☐ Starlog
- ☐ Wired
- ☐ Vice
- ☐ BPM
- ☐ I hate reading
- ☐ Other:_____

4. Have you visited the ADV Manga website?
- ☐ Yes
- ☐ No

5. Have you made any Manga purchases online from the ADV website?
- ☐ Yes
- ☐ No

6. If you have visited the ADV Manga website, how would you rate your online experience?
- ☐ Excellent
- ☐ Good
- ☐ Average
- ☐ Poor

7. What genre of Manga do you prefer?
(Check all that apply)
- ☐ adventure
- ☐ romance
- ☐ detective
- ☐ action
- ☐ horror
- ☐ sci-fi/fantasy
- ☐ sports
- ☐ comedy

8. How many manga titles have you purchased in the last 6 months?
- ☐ none
- ☐ 1-4
- ☐ 5-10
- ☐ 11+

9. Where do you make your manga purchases? *(Check all that apply)*
- ☐ comic store
- ☐ bookstore
- ☐ newsstand
- ☐ online
- ☐ other:_____
- ☐ department store
- ☐ grocery store
- ☐ video store
- ☐ video game store

10. Which bookstores do you usually make your manga purchases at?
- ☐ Barnes & Noble
- ☐ Walden Books
- ☐ Suncoast
- ☐ Best Buy
- ☐ Amazon.com
- ☐ Borders
- ☐ Books-A-Million
- ☑ Toys "Я" Us
- ☐ Other bookstore: _____

11. What's your favorite anime/manga website?
- ☐ adv-manga.com
- ☐ advfilms.com
- ☐ rightstuf.com
- ☐ animenewsservice.com
- ☐ animenewsnetwork.com
- ☐ Other:_____
- ☐ animeondvd.com
- ☐ anipike.com
- ☐ animeonline.net
- ☐ planetanime.com
- ☐ animenation.com